The Original
Summer Bridge Activities™

Sixth to Seventh Grade

SBA was created by
Michele D. Van Leeuwen

written by
Dr. Leland Graham
Frankie Long

illustrations by
Magen Mitchell
Amanda Sorensen

Summer Learning Staff
Clareen Arnold, Lori Davis, Melody Feist, Aimee Hansen, Christopher Kugler, Kristina Kugler, Molly McMahon, Paul Rawlins, Liza Richards, Linda Swain

Design
Andy Carlson, Robyn Funk

Cover Art
John Shroades

ISBN: 1-59441-732-6

20 19 18 17 16 15 14 13 12 11 10 9 8 7

Dear Parents,

The summer months are a perfect time to reconnect with your young scholar on many levels after a long school year. Your personal involvement is so important to your child's immediate and long-term academic success. No matter how wonderful your child's classroom experience is, your involvement outside the classroom will make it that much better!

Summer Bridge Activities™ is the original summer workbook developed to help parents support their children academically while away from school, and we strive to improve the content, the activities, and the resources to give you the highest quality summer learning materials available. Ten years ago, we introduced **Summer Bridge Activities™** to a small group of teachers and parents after I had successfully used it to help my own child prepare for the new school year. It was a hit then, and it continues to be a hit now! Many other summer workbooks have been introduced since, but **Summer Bridge Activities™** continues to be the one that both teachers and parents ask for most. We take our responsibility as the leader in summer education seriously and are always looking for new ways to make summer learning more fun, more motivating, and more effective to help make your child's transition to the new school year enjoyable and successful!

We are now excited to offer you even more bonus summer learning materials online at www.SummerBridgeActivities.com! This site has great resources for both parents and kids to use on their own and together. An expanded summer reading program where kids can post their own book reviews, writing and reading contests with great prizes, assessment tests, travel packs, and even games are a few of the additional resources that you and your child will have access to with the included **Summer Bridge Activities™** Online Pass Code.

Summer Learning has come a long way over the last 10 years, and we are glad that you have chosen to use **Summer Bridge Activities™** to help your children continue to discover the world around them by using the classroom skills they worked so hard to obtain!

Have a wonderful summer!

Michele Van Leeuwen and the Summer Learning Staff!

Hey Kids!

We bet you had a great school year! Congratulations on all your hard work! We just want to say that we're proud of the great things you did this year, and we're excited to have you spend time with us over the summer. Have fun with your **Summer Bridge Activities™** workbook, and visit us online at www.SummerBridgeActivities.com for more fun, cool, and exciting stuff!

Have a great summer!

The T.O.C. (Table of Contents)

Official Pass Code

ac0226c

Log on to **www.SummerBridgeActivities.com** and join!

Sections of SBA

- There are three sections in SBA: the first and second review, the third previews.

- Each section begins with an SBA Motivational Calendar.

- Each day your child will complete activities in reading, writing, math, language, science, or social studies. The activities become progressively more challenging.

- Each page is numbered by day.

Here's what you will find inside

Summer Bridge Activities™

Exercises in **Summer Bridge Activities™** (SBA) are easy to understand and presented in fun and creative ways that motivate students to review familiar skills while being progressively challenged. In addition to basic skills in reading, writing, math, and language arts, **Summer Bridge Activities™** contains activities that challenge and reinforce skills in geography and science!

Daily exercises review and preview skills in reading, writing, math, language arts, social studies, and science. Exercises cover 2 subjects per day and are divided into 3 sections to correlate with traditional summer vacation.

Science pages provide hands-on science exercises.

A Summer Reading List introduces some of today's popular titles as well as the classics. Kids can rate books they read and log on to www.**SummerBridgeActivities**.com to post reviews, find more great titles, and participate in national reading and writing contests!

Motivational Calendars begin each section to help motivate kids all summer long.

Removable Answer Pages ensure that parents know as much as their kids!

A Certificate of Completion for parents to sign congratulates summer learners for their work and welcomes them to the grade ahead.

A grade-appropriate, official Summer Fun pass code gives kids and parents online access to more bonus games, contests, and resources at www.**SummerBridgeActivities**.com.

Here are some groups who say our books are great!

Mr. Fredrickson

Maximizing
The Original Summer Bridge Activities™

Let your middle-grade student familiarize himself with the workbook. Have him look through the pages to see what skills and exercises the book contains as well as how the book is formatted.

Agree on a time that your child will complete the daily exercises. Make sure that it is consistent and that it is a set amount of time.

Provide any necessary materials, including a pencil, ruler, dictionary, or other reference books. In addition, be prepared to use the Internet, as some activities may contain material that students need to research online.

Support your young scholar with positive guidance and direction. The activities are not meant to be tests, but rather re-enforcement. Remain positive and supportive as your child dedicates time during the summer.

Encourage your child to complete the exercises on her own or to research the material online before coming to you. However, be there if she needs you.

Encourage summertime reading! Students may get tired of reading textbooks during the school year, so use the summer months to remind them how great reading for pleasure and entertainment is!

Above all, remember to have fun with learning during the summer! You and your young scholar are being proactive with education, and you should enjoy the experience of learning outside of the classroom!

Social Skills ...

Be Honest with Yourself and Other People. Dishonesty may work for a little while, but it will catch up with you and soon be discovered. Your integrity is vital to your self-worth. Value yourself and others will.

Have Pride in Yourself. There is no point in trying to be different from who you really are. Others will find out what you are like anyway. There may be things you want to improve on to become a better person, but be proud of who you are. No one likes a phony.

Stay True to Your Principles. Don't give up what you believe in to make friends. Think about what you believe in, be confident in yourself, and know why you believe this way. You do not have to change just so someone will like you.

Lend a Listening Ear. Listening to others makes them feel good and important. Look them in the eyes. Give them your full attention. By listening, you compliment them, and they will like you for that.

Seek Common Ground. The places you go determine the kind of people you will meet. Get out and mix with others. Introduce yourself. Keep in mind that most people are just as cautious as you are about meeting people. Generally, they will be glad you spoke first.

Dress to Impress. When you go out, others will notice your general appearance before you even have a chance to speak. Take pride in yourself and how you look.

Remember Names & Faces. Follow these three simple steps:
  a. Listen to the name so you can remember it. If you were unable to catch the person's name the first time, ask again—that is a compliment. It shows that you are interested.
  b. In your conversation, call the person by name as soon as possible. This will help you remember.
  c. Picture the person's name spelled out in your mind, with his or her face in the background, or relate the name to something familiar to help you remember.

Talk with Confidence in Your Voice. When you use your voice, be kind, clear, and enthusiastic. Avoid being a loudmouth, and include others in conversation. You will make friends by making others feel part of the activity.

and Self-Worth

Have Personality. Smile—you will win friends. Have a sense of humor—everyone needs to laugh. Friendship is all about having fun!

Lend a Helping Hand. You'll be admired for your kindness. Politeness shows respect for others.

Initiate a Conversation. Talk about famous people, your favorite athletes, or current events.

Keep the Conversation Alive. Find out what the other person's interests are. Ask questions like: "What do you like doing after school?" "Where were you born?" "What is your favorite movie?" These types of questions require more than just "yes" or "no" answers. Listen to the response. Look for things that both of you have a common interest in to keep the conversation alive.

Everybody Has an Opinion. Share your opinions, but respect other people's right to have their own opinions, which may be different than yours.

Don't Burden Others. When trying to develop a friendship, keep your problems to yourself until a later time. Forcing your burdens on someone may scare your new friend away.

Respect Privacy. Talk about common interests, but don't pry into the other person's private life.

Don't Be a Gossiper. When you gossip, you hurt others as well as yourself. People who gossip lose the trust of others and may lose the chance to make new friends.

Have Confidence in Yourself. Share your accomplishments, but don't brag or boast (praise yourself or your possessions). Nothing will turn someone away faster than bragging.

Be Positive with Your Friends. Build up your friends by complimenting them on their strengths instead of tearing them down in front of others. Everybody has weaknesses, including you. With a friend's support, weaknesses can become strengths. People like to be around others who make them feel good about themselves and the company they keep.

Summertime = Reading Time!

Your young scholars are now at a place where reading should be an activity that they do on a regular basis. It is important that they know how to explore books, titles, and authors and understand where they can go to find books and other reading materials. As adults we often assume that our children know where to go because of their involvement in school activities and programs; however, we need to support and encourage their love of reading at home as well.

Books to Read

The Summer Reading List has a variety of titles, including some found in the Accelerated Reader Program.

We recommend parents read to pre-kindergarten through 1st grade children 5–10 minutes each day and then ask questions about the story to reinforce comprehension. For higher grade levels, we suggest the following daily reading times: grades 1–2, 10–20 min.; grades 2–3, 20–30 min.; grades 3–4, 30–45 min.; grades 4–8, 45–60 min.

It is important to decide an amount of reading time and write it on the SBA Motivational Calendar.

Here are a few ideas on encouraging reading in your middle-grade students this summer and fostering more enthusiasm for the adventure of reading outside the classroom.

Lead by example! Show your kids how much you enjoy reading by doing it yourself. Curl up with a book where your kids can see you reading—and enjoying it!

Ask your children thought-provoking questions about topics that interest them, and encourage them to explore them through books! Have them research titles online and go to the bookstore or library to check out the books they found.

Talk to your children about books that you were interested in when you were their age. You may even find that they have heard of some of the same books!

Form a reading group and take turns choosing books to read. Give yourselves a couple of weeks or even a month to read, and then plan a lunch or dinner where you can discuss the book with each other.

Look for programs offered by your local library. These don't need to have anything to do with reading but can be talks about local artists, film, and even authors themselves. Get your kids interested in topics that they will want to learn more about, and encourage them to find out more on their own through books and literature.

Summer Bridge Activities™

Summer Reading List

Fill in the stars and rate your favorite (and not so favorite) books here and online at
www.SummerBridgeActivities.com!

1 = I struggled to finish this book.
2 = I thought this book was pretty good.
3 = I thought this book rocked!
4 = I want to read this book again and again!

Ada, Alma Flor ☆☆☆☆

**Under the Royal Palms:
A Childhood in Cuba**

Adler, C.S. ☆☆☆☆

Tuna Fish Thanksgiving

Alphin, Elaine ☆☆☆☆

Ghost Cadet

Amoss, Berthe ☆☆☆☆

Lost Magic

Babbitt, Natalie ☆☆☆☆

Tuck Everlasting

Birdseye, Tom ☆☆☆☆

Tucker

Brashares, Ann 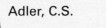 4

The Sisterhood of the Traveling Pants

Brittain, Bill ☆☆☆☆

The Wish Giver

Cabot, Meg ☆☆☆☆

The Princess Diaries

Curtis, Christopher Paul  4

Bud, Not Buddy ☆☆☆☆

Cushman, Karen ☆☆☆☆

Catherine, Called Birdy

Dahl, Roald ☆☆☆☆ 4

Charlie and the Chocolate Factory

Durbin, William ☆☆☆☆

The Broken Blade

Eckart, Allan W. ☆☆☆☆

Incident at Hawk's Hill

Farmer, Nancy ☆☆☆☆☆
The House of the Scorpion

Paolini, Christopher ☆☆☆☆☆ 3
Eragon

Fleischman, Paul ☆☆☆☆☆
The Borning Room

Paulsen, Gary ☆☆☆☆
Tracker

Haddix, Margaret Peterson ☆☆☆☆☆ 4
Among the Hidden

Philbrick, Rodman ☆☆☆☆☆
The Last Book in the Universe

Jelloun, Tahar Ben ☆☆☆☆☆
Islam Explained

Rodda, Emily ☆☆☆☆☆
Dragons of Deltora

Lowry, Lois ☆☆☆☆☆
Gathering Blue

Soto, Gary ☆☆☆☆☆
Taking Sides

Montgomery, L. M. ☆☆☆☆☆
Anne of Green Gables

Staples, Suzanne Fisher ☆☆☆☆☆
Shabanu, Daughter of the Wind

Morris, Gerald ☆☆☆☆☆
The Squire's Tale

Tolan, Stephanie S. ☆☆☆☆☆
Surviving the Applewhites

Morpurgo, Michael ☆☆☆☆☆
Waiting for Anya

Tolkien, J.R.R. ☆☆☆☆☆ 4
The Hobbit

O'Brien, Robert C. ☆☆☆☆☆
Z for Zachariah

Join the SBA Kids Summer Reading Club!

**Quick! Get Mom or Dad to help you log on and
join the SBA Kids Summer Reading Club. You can
find more great books, tell your friends about your
favorite titles, and even win cool prizes! Log on to
www.SummerBridgeActivities.com and sign up today.**

Incentive Contract Calendar

Month _____

My parents and I decided that if I complete 15 days of
Summer Bridge Activities™ 6–7 and read _____ minutes a day,
my incentive/reward will be:

_____

Child's Signature_____

Parent's Signature_____

EXAMPLE: ☑ ☑ _AC_

Day 1 ☐ ☐ _____   Day 8 ☐ ☐ _____

Day 2 ☐ ☐ _____   Day 9 ☐ ☐ _____

Day 3 ☐ ☐ _____   Day 10 ☐ ☐ _____

Day 4 ☐ ☐ _____   Day 11 ☐ ☐ _____

Day 5 ☐ ☐ _____   Day 12 ☐ ☐ _____

Day 6 ☐ ☐ _____   Day 13 ☐ ☐ _____

Day 7 ☐ ☐ _____   Day 14 ☐ ☐ _____

                       Day 15 ☐ ☐ _____

Child: Put a ✔ in the ☐ for the daily activities [notebook] completed.

         Put a ✔ in the ☐ for the daily reading [book] completed.

Parent: Initial the ____ for daily activities and reading your child completes.

My plans for the Summer!

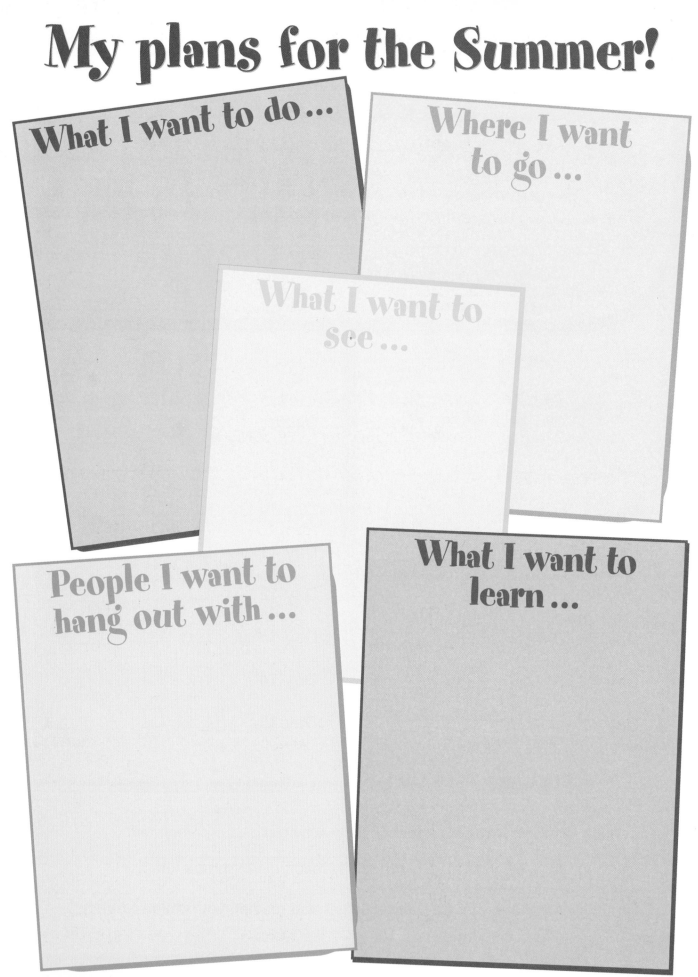

What I want to do …

Where I want to go …

What I want to see …

People I want to hang out with …

What I want to learn …

Latitude and Longitude

Remember, lines extending east and west are called lines of *latitude*. Lines extending north and south are called lines of *longitude*. All of North America is located in the Northern Hemisphere, north of the equator, which is located at 0° latitude. North America is also located in the Western Hemisphere, west of the prime meridian, which is 0° longitude. Together, lines of latitude and longitude comprise the *global grid*. The global grid helps to locate any place on earth. If you know the approximate latitude and longitude of a location, you can find it on a map. For this exercise, use the map on page 114.

Use the map on page 114 to match the following locations:

e	1. Victoria Island	A. 20°N, 100°W
g	2. Baffin Island	B. 09°N, 80°W
c	3. Newfoundland	C. 49°N, 56°W
i	4. Cuba	D. 10°N, 84°W
b	5. Panama Canal	E. 70°N, 110°W
a	6. Mexico City, Mexico	F. 30°N, 90°W
h	7. Vancouver, B.C.	G. 70°N, 72°W
f	8. New Orleans, LA	H. 48°N, 123°W
d	9. San José, Costa Rica	I. 22°N, 80°W
j	10. Bahamas	J. 25°N, 78°W

Biology Crossword. Miranda, the botanist, headed to the jungle to search for new plant species. She found a strange fungus growing on a log. The squishy growth resembled a fungus that was supposed to be extinct. Many plants Miranda had never seen before surrounded the fungus. Miranda got to work classifying the plants. She decided that the fungus was an adaptation of the original species. It was now a vital part of the local biosphere. The fungus decomposed dead vegetation and returned valuable nutrients to the soil. This allowed plant and animal kingdoms in the area to thrive. Miranda knew this patch of land would be valuable for other researchers trying to save species and preserve biodiversity in their areas.

classifying	kingdom	fungus
adaptation	extinct	plant
biosphere	species	biodiversity
botanist	animal	

Across:

2. living organisms and the environment they live in

6. a member of a kingdom of living things that have many cells, can move and sense their environments, but do not make their own food.

7. a scientist that studies plants

10. a group of living things that have certain similar characteristics

Down:

1. grouping things together

3. no longer living or existing

4. a member of a kingdom of living things that resemble plants but do not have leaves or flowers

5. a member of a kingdom of living things that do not move about but do make their own food

7. the variety and number of living things in a specific area

8. a change that helps a living thing survive in its environment

9. the largest category in the classification of living things

Read each phrase below. Fill in the bubble for the word that has the same or almost the same meaning (*synonym*) as the underlined word.

1. <u>significant</u> detection
   - ◉ A. surprising
   - ○ B. fruitful
   - ○ C. important
   - ○ D. extended

2. quick <u>response</u>
   - ○ A. bargain
   - ◉ B. answer
   - ○ C. calmness
   - ○ D. detail

3. <u>vacant</u> building
   - ○ A. empty
   - ○ B. involved
   - ○ C. crowded
   - ○ D. noisy

4. <u>irritate</u> your sister
   - ○ A. interview
   - ◉ B. annoy
   - ○ C. pursue
   - ○ D. enjoy

5. <u>champion</u> a cause
   - ◉ A. overcome
   - ○ B. maintain
   - ○ C. confront
   - ○ D. defend

6. <u>complete</u> my work
   - ◉ A. finish
   - ○ B. fake
   - ○ C. lose
   - ○ D. promise

7. <u>miserable</u> cold
   - ○ A. tired
   - ○ B. cheerful
   - ◉ C. terrible
   - ○ D. agreeable

8. <u>thorough</u> report
   - ○ A. incomplete
   - ○ B. complete
   - ○ C. average
   - ○ D. typical

9. <u>reside</u> in New Jersey
   - ○ A. search
   - ○ B. visit
   - ○ C. enter
   - ○ D. live

Rewrite the paragraphs below. They contain sentence fragments and run-on sentences. Decide where the sentences should be separated. Add punctuation marks and capitals.

Music and Dancing

In the past. People in Europe and America danced their traditional folk dances at fairs, festivals, weddings and celebrations, folk dances are very old, and the steps have been passed down from parents to children for hundreds of years. Today they are mostly performed by dance groups. In national costumes.

In other parts of the world. People have traditional dances. That they perform at festivals or use to tell stories. Of their gods and heroes.

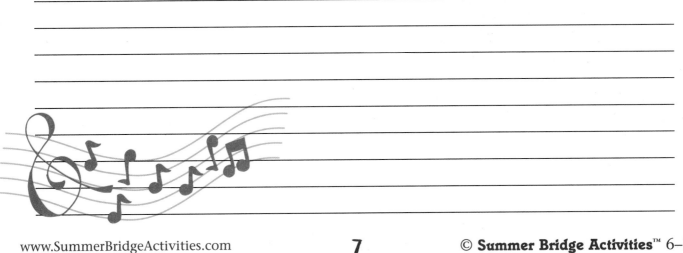

Day 3

Multiples and Least Common Multiples

1. Coco's Bake Shop sells pastries in groups of 4 and cookies by the half dozen (6). What is the least number of each you would need to buy in order to have an equal number of pastries and cookies? _____

List the next five multiples of each number.

2. 2 _____

3. 16 _____

4. 7 _____

5. 25 _____

6. 10 _____

7. 150 _____

Write the LCM (least common multiple) of the numbers.

8. 2 and 5 __10__

9. 8 and 12 _____

10. 5 and 7 __35__

11. 2, 3, and 5 _____

12. 6 and 8 __48__

13. 3, 10, and 15 _____

A year whose number is divisible by 4 is a leap year. A number is divisible by 4 if the number formed by its last two digits is divisible by 4. The only exception is that a century year is a leap year only when its number is divisible by 400. Is the year a leap year? Write Yes or No.

14. 1812   15. 1992   16. 2100   17. 1882   18. 1900

Challenge

If you were to live to be 80 years old, how many leap years would you see?

A Character Sketch

A character sketch is a description of a real or imaginary person. Select one of your friends to write about. Describe your friend's appearance. Include some of your friend's favorite things. What are some interesting facts about your friend? What are some things that your friend does not like? When you finish, check your spelling, punctuation, and capitalization.

_____   _____

_____   _____

_____   _____

_____   _____

_____   _____

_____   _____

_____   _____

_____   _____

_____   _____

_____   _____

_____

_____

The subject and verb in a sentence must agree in number. Read the sentences below and then underline the subject and circle the verb. Write S in the blank if the subject is *singular*. Write P if it is *plural*. Write C if it is collective (team, crowd).

run   1. The boys (run, runs) around the track every day during P.E.

plays   2. The girls' basketball team (play, plays) hard every Thursday night.

_____   3. Toni and her sister (rides, ride) the school bus every day except Friday.

_____   4. Our school band (practices, practice) after school three times a week.

_____   5. You (was, were) really lucky to have seen the last hockey game of the season.

_____   6. They (have, has) decided to jog around the track after school each day.

_____   7. The ten girls (is, are) going to the neighborhood swimming party next Sunday.

_____   8. The science fair judging (was, were) held on Thursday in the gymnasium.

_____   9. Who can guess how many pennies (is, are) in this fishbowl?

_____ 10. The football crowd always (stand, stands) for the national anthem.

Factors and Greatest Common Factors. When one number is divisible by a second, the second number is called a *factor* of the first. Two numbers may have some factors that are the same. These numbers are called common factors. The greatest of the common factors of two numbers is called their greatest common factor (GCF). Complete the following:

1. factors of 4: __ __ __

2. factors of 16: __ __ __ __ __

    factors of 8: __ __ __ __

    factors of 20: __ __ __ __ __ __

    common factors of 4 and 8: __ __ __

    common factors of 16 and 20: __ __ __

    GCF of 4 and 8: __

    GCF of 16 and 20: __

Write the GCF of the numbers.

3. 5 and 15 _____

6. 18 and 21 _____

9. 15 and 18 _____

4. 12 and 24 _____

7. 7 and 15 _____

10. 15 and 40 _____

5. 4 and 6 __12__

8. 12 and 44 _____

11. 13 and 21 _____

Challenge

12. There are 12 teachers and 42 students competing in the Student-Faculty Meet. How many players per team will there be if (a) the teacher teams and the student teams must have the same number of students and faculty, and (b) the teams are as large as possible? How many teams in all?

Calculators Please

13. The number **496** has nine factors besides 496. The sum of these nine factors is 496. What are the nine factors?

Regions. Identify the numbered state and its capital from the Southern Region. Use an atlas for assistance.

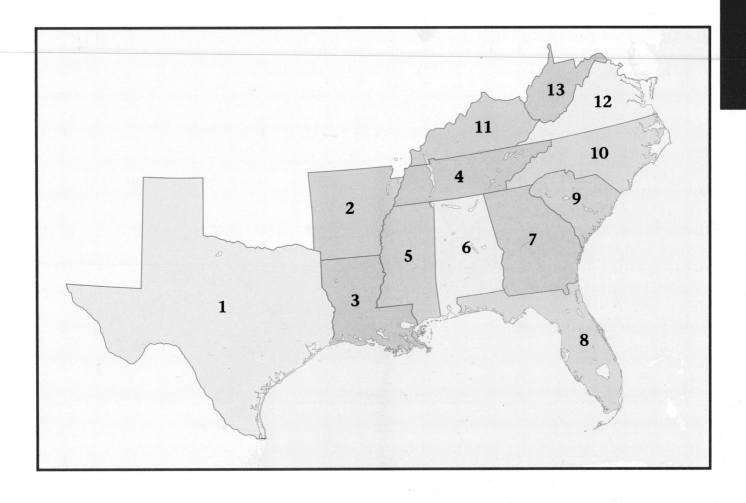

Which state is located between each of the two states named?

Louisiana	Mississippi	Alabama
Kentucky	West Virginia	Virginia
Alabama	Georgia	South Carolina
Florida	Alabama	Mississippi
West Virginia	Virginia	North Carolina
Mississippi	Tennese	Kentucky
Georgia	Southcarolina	North Carolina
Tennessee	North Carolina	South Carolina
Texas	Louisiana	Mississippi
Arkansas	Tennese	North Carolina

The Water Cycle. More than two-thirds of the Earth's surface is covered with water, and the cells of most living creatures are about 70 percent water. Water travels in a constant cycle. This cycle is necessary for all life, and it keeps our atmosphere and planet healthy. Energy from the sun causes water in Earth's oceans to evaporate. Hot air rises and carries water vapor up into the cooler atmosphere. Here water vapor forms clouds. Water falls from the clouds as rain or snow. This is called precipitation. Both plants and animals use or store some water and return the rest to the environment. Plants release water through their leaves. Animals release water with their waste products. The ground absorbs some of this water, and the rest is evaporated by the sun, continuing the cycle.

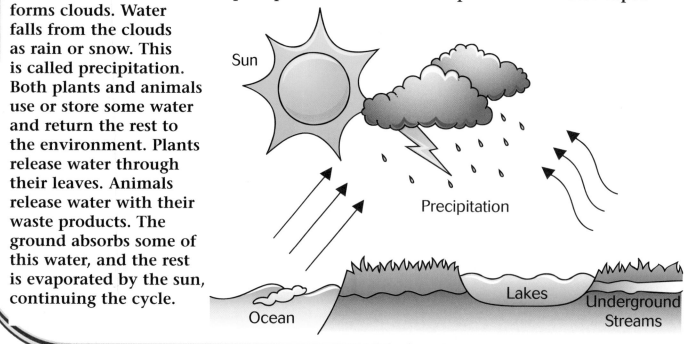

The answer to each of the questions below is included in the word search. Fill in the blanks and then circle the words in the puzzle.

```
y p a p s d l n i m g c u r
y o m j f c b u u x v l z u
h c i u e e l s q n s i y n
q b r t n k u y q b d s f d
n a e c o j n f r o z e n e
u y z i k r a o i n y s h r
r a c j u q s y c h s r f n
h p r m q b y g j p w k r e
i i y r a s s e c e n w p a
x r e t a w d a y l i g h t
n o i t a t i p i c e r p h
g j g h j q i s d u o l c h
d t t p o h n h e j t p w p
g e l c y c h s s k m v a o
```

WATER CYCLE CLUES

1. Rivers empty into the _____
2. The earth has more water than land.
3. Water cycles are _____ for all life.
4. Water travels in a _____.
5. The _____ are really water vapor.
6. Springs come from _____ the ground.
7. The ground _____ water.
8. The _____ evaporates water.
9. Most evaporation occurs during ____ hours.
10. Water falls to the earth in the form of _____.

Each sentence is followed by a pair of *homophones* (words that sound alike). Fill in the blank with the word that best completes the meaning of the sentence. If there are two blanks in a sentence, write the correct word in its corresponding blank.

1. My little sister was totally _____ with the baseball game.   board/bored

2. Mrs. Cook told our class that we sounded like a _____ of buffalo.   heard/herd

3. _____ completing the questions on the test now.   They're/Their

4. Visitors to the school are not _____ in this area.   allowed/aloud

5. My best friend and I _____ the mathematics test.   passed/past

6. Our family stayed in the luxury hotel _____ where all the
   guests were provided _____ chocolates at night.   sweet/suite

7. I don't know _____ we should go to the picnic because of
   the approaching _____ conditions.   weather/whether

8. When the _____ toured our part of the building, he stated
   his main _____, or rule, of conduct.   principal/principle

9. _____ your name at the top of your paper when you finish.   Write/Right

10. The cheerleaders printed the sign in all _____ letters.   capital/capitol

A *prepositional phrase* is a group of words that begins with a preposition (such as *of*, *in*, *between*) and ends with a noun or pronoun. Underline the prepositional phrases in the following sentences.

Need Help? Check Out Grammar Links at www.SummerBridgeActivities.com

11. My older sister received a love letter from her new
    boyfriend.

12. Mrs. Powell's sixth grade class enjoyed learning about the Oregon Trail.

13. Last summer my family and I went on vacation to the Grand Canyon.

14. Students, you may use your calculators for the problems on this test.

15. The impatient driver behind us continued to honk his horn.

16. I believe I saw your science book underneath your coat.

17. My mother always eats a banana in the morning with breakfast and an apple with lunch.

18. The new clothing store is around the corner and across the street from the dry cleaners.

Equivalent Fractions. All fractions that name the same number are called *equivalent fractions* ($\frac{1}{5} = \frac{2}{10} = \frac{10}{50}$). Equivalent fractions are determined or created by multiplying or dividing both the numerator and denominator by the same number.

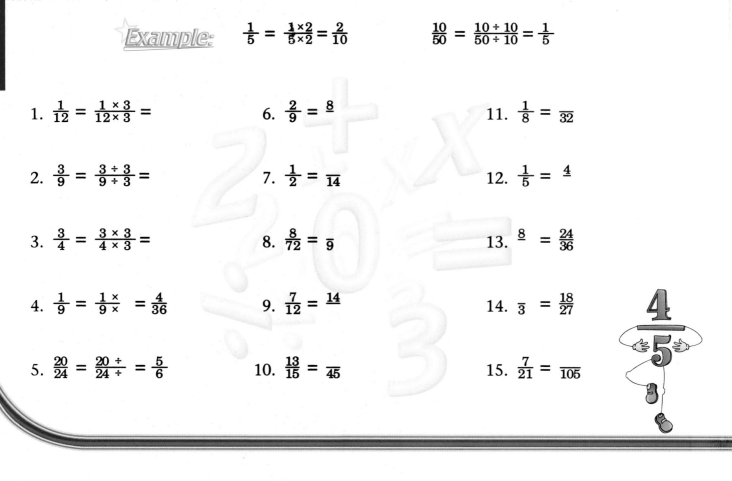

Example: $\frac{1}{5} = \frac{1 \times 2}{5 \times 2} = \frac{2}{10}$ $\frac{10}{50} = \frac{10 \div 10}{50 \div 10} = \frac{1}{5}$

1. $\frac{1}{12} = \frac{1 \times 3}{12 \times 3} = $

2. $\frac{3}{9} = \frac{3 \div 3}{9 \div 3} = $

3. $\frac{3}{4} = \frac{3 \times 3}{4 \times 3} = $

4. $\frac{1}{9} = \frac{1 \times}{9 \times} = \frac{4}{36}$

5. $\frac{20}{24} = \frac{20 \div}{24 \div} = \frac{5}{6}$

6. $\frac{2}{9} = \frac{8}{}$

7. $\frac{1}{2} = \frac{}{14}$

8. $\frac{8}{72} = \frac{}{9}$

9. $\frac{7}{12} = \frac{14}{}$

10. $\frac{13}{15} = \frac{}{45}$

11. $\frac{1}{8} = \frac{}{32}$

12. $\frac{1}{5} = \frac{4}{}$

13. $\frac{8}{} = \frac{24}{36}$

14. $\frac{}{3} = \frac{18}{27}$

15. $\frac{7}{21} = \frac{}{105}$

Indicate the two equivalent fractions in each problem by circling them.

16. $\frac{6}{10}$, $\frac{6}{8}$, $\frac{3}{5}$, $\frac{4}{10}$

17. $\frac{3}{12}$, $\frac{1}{12}$, $\frac{1}{3}$, $\frac{1}{4}$

18. $\frac{7}{8}$, $\frac{14}{17}$, $\frac{28}{32}$, $\frac{36}{40}$

19. $\frac{13}{26}$, $\frac{13}{39}$, $\frac{1}{13}$, $\frac{1}{2}$

20. $\frac{6}{10}$, $\frac{11}{20}$, $\frac{22}{40}$, $\frac{26}{40}$

21. $\frac{1}{2}$, $\frac{3}{8}$, $\frac{5}{12}$, $\frac{18}{48}$

22. $\frac{2}{9}$, $\frac{1}{6}$, $\frac{6}{54}$, $\frac{4}{18}$

23. $\frac{13}{14}$, $\frac{16}{28}$, $\frac{6}{7}$, $\frac{26}{28}$

24. $\frac{5}{7}$, $\frac{11}{15}$, $\frac{30}{35}$, $\frac{33}{45}$

The Compound Sentence. A *compound sentence* is made up of two or more simple sentences, usually joined by a connecting word. The words *and, but, or, nor, for,* or *yet* are used to connect the simple sentences. If a sentence below is simple, write S. If a sentence is compound, write C.

_____ 1. My little sister is only five years old, and she loves to play with her dolls all day.

_____ 2. It is very important to always listen to what is being said in class.

_____ 3. I do not like cats, but my mother and sister love them.

_____ 4. My two shelties always wait for me to walk them in the afternoon.

_____ 5. The students had worked hard on the science projects, but they did not win any prizes.

_____ 6. Mrs. Walker told our class to complete the research papers by Friday.

_____ 7. Mr. Thomas and Ms. Edwards volunteered to help serve the refreshments at the meeting.

_____ 8. Please board the ship as soon as possible, and present your ticket to the attendant.

_____ 9. My dad and I built a doghouse, but our dog would not stay in it.

_____ 10. My cousins and their parents plan to visit us this summer.

Choosing *Who* and *Whom*. *Who* generally is used as a subject. *Whom* is used as an object. Complete each sentence below with *who* or *whom*.

11. From _____ have you received invitations to the Christmas parties?

12. There are a lot of students _____ really like our new math teacher, Mr. Watkins.

13. _____ do you students know in San Diego, California?

14. Everyone in the courtroom wondered _____ the mysterious witness would be.

15. If I had known _____ he was, I would have been more friendly.

16. The two men _____ the police arrested for a parking ticket were wanted for robbery.

17. I do not remember to _____ I lent my science book.

18. Philip Anderson is a student _____, I think, is really qualified for president of our class.

19. No one has figured out to _____ the teacher was referring.

20. I wonder _____ sent me this wonderful birthday card.

Need Help?
Check Out
Grammar Links at
www.SummerBridgeActivities.com

Cross Products. Cross products may be used to check if two fractions are equivalent. When cross products are equal, the fractions are equivalent.

Example: $\frac{2}{9}$, $\frac{4}{18}$ → $\frac{2}{9} \times \frac{4}{18}$ → $2 \times 18 \qquad 9 \times 4$

$$36 \quad = \quad 36$$

Check the cross products for equivalent fractions.

1. $\frac{3}{4}$, $\frac{9}{12}$ 　　　　2. $\frac{2}{5}$, $\frac{21}{30}$ 　　　　3. $\frac{1}{6}$, $\frac{2}{18}$

4. $\frac{5}{9}$, $\frac{20}{36}$ 　　　　5. $\frac{7}{9}$, $\frac{35}{40}$ 　　　　6. $\frac{8}{15}$, $\frac{24}{45}$

Comparing Fractions. To compare fractions with like denominators, compare their numerators. To compare fractions with unlike denominators, rewrite fractions as fractions with a common denominator.

A common denominator is a common multiple of the denominators. The least common denominator (LCD) is the least common multiple (LCM) of the denominators.

Example: $\frac{2}{3}$　$\frac{3}{4}$

Rewrite as fractions with a common denominator.

$$\frac{2}{3} = \frac{8}{12} \qquad \frac{3}{4} = \frac{9}{12}$$

Compare the fractions.

$$\frac{8}{12} < \frac{9}{12} \quad \text{so} \quad \frac{2}{3} < \frac{3}{4}$$

Rewrite the fractions. Use the LCD for each pair.

7. $\frac{5}{6}$, $\frac{11}{12}$ → $\frac{10}{12}$, $\frac{11}{12}$　8. $\frac{1}{3}$, $\frac{2}{5}$ 　　　9. $\frac{1}{4}$, $\frac{3}{10}$ 　　　10. $\frac{4}{11}$, $\frac{3}{33}$

11. $\frac{1}{10}$, $\frac{4}{15}$ 　　　12. $\frac{1}{3}$, $\frac{2}{9}$ 　　　13. $\frac{3}{5}$, $\frac{4}{9}$ 　　　14. $\frac{1}{7}$, $\frac{5}{9}$

Write < or > to compare the fractions.

15. $\frac{7}{7}$　$\frac{4}{7}$ 　　16. $\frac{7}{8}$　$\frac{3}{4}$ 　　17. $\frac{1}{3}$　$\frac{7}{12}$ 　　18. $\frac{1}{2}$　$\frac{5}{8}$

Today, many people move every few years. Of course, by moving often, people can experience different places, friends, and climates. Other people prefer to stay in one place all their lives and never move far from home. Write a paragraph stating whether you think it is better to stay in one place or to move often and live in different places.

_____

_____

_____

_____

_____

_____

_____

_____

_____

_____

_____

_____

_____

_____

An *adverb* is a word that modifies a verb, an adjective, or another adverb. Underline the adverb in each sentence; then write the word that the adverb modifies.

1. Tommy really likes his new part-time job.   _____

2. Willie always goes to basketball practice after school.   _____

3. Mrs. Campbell never gives tests on Fridays.   _____

4. The old house at the end of the street burned quickly.   _____

5. Since Bryan was very tired, he decided to go to bed.   _____

6. Sherry studied hard for her math test.   _____

7. Monica and her news staff work quickly to gather the daily news _____

8. Heather was too tired to write her research report last night.   _____

9. Suddenly, he heard a loud noise from the garage.   _____

10. Roger worked all the math problems easily.   _____

Write < or > to compare the fractions.

1. $\frac{1}{7}$ $\frac{4}{7}$ 2. $\frac{3}{8}$ $\frac{3}{4}$ 3. $\frac{1}{3}$ $\frac{1}{12}$ 4. $\frac{1}{2}$ $\frac{1}{8}$

   $\frac{2}{7}$ $\frac{4}{7}$ $\frac{5}{8}$ $\frac{3}{4}$ $\frac{1}{3}$ $\frac{5}{12}$ $\frac{1}{2}$ $\frac{3}{8}$

5. Tony spent $\frac{2}{3}$ of an hour on the Internet and $\frac{7}{8}$ of an hour watching television. On which activity did he spend more time?

6. Margaret completed $\frac{1}{4}$ of her project on Wednesday and another $\frac{1}{3}$ of the project on Friday. On which day did she complete more of her project?

7. Angela cooked $\frac{2}{5}$ of a pound of rice on Friday and $\frac{3}{7}$ of a pound on Saturday. On which day did she cook the most rice?

Fractions. Simplify to lowest term. To simplify $\frac{6}{12}$, divide the numerator and denominator by the Greatest Common Factor (GCF) of the two numbers.

Example: $\frac{6}{12} = \frac{6 \div 6}{12 \div 6} = \frac{1}{2}$

Simplify.

1. $\frac{2}{6}$ $\frac{2 \div 2}{6 \div 2} = \frac{1}{3}$ 4. $\frac{9}{36}$ 7. $\frac{35}{50}$

2. $\frac{8}{40}$ 5. $\frac{14}{28}$ 8. $\frac{15}{54}$

3. $\frac{7}{28}$ 6. $\frac{14}{21}$ 9. $\frac{16}{40}$

These are facts that a news reporter learned while reporting on a story down on the water front. Write the fractions in lowest terms.

10. The ice in the harbor is able to float because it is only $\frac{900}{1000}$ as heavy as water.

11. On an average fishing boat, $\frac{580}{720}$ of the day's catch was unusable.

12. On one of the larger cruise ships, $\frac{126}{2394}$ passengers were from a foreign country.

United States Government. The U.S. Constitution guarantees a balance of power between the three branches of the government at all levels of the government. Fill in a branch of the government on each of the capitol steps.

Need Help? Check Out Social Science Links at www.SummerBridgeActivities.com

1. _____

2. _____

3. _____

Fill in the chart below describing who each branch of government includes, what the branch's responsibilities are, and how each branch carries these out.

BRANCH   _____   _____   _____

WHO   _____   _____   _____

WHAT   _____   _____   _____
         _____   _____   _____

HOW   _____   _____   _____
         _____   _____   _____
         _____   _____   _____

Growing Crystals. Crystals are regularly shaped, repeating units of a substance. Some crystals are unique in shape and formation. This experiment in crystal-growing must be carried out in the open air or in a well-ventilated room.

Materials:

12–18 charcoal briquettes (plain, no lighter fluid)
thick paper bag
hammer
measuring cup
1 cup laundry bluing (use liquid or mix up enough to make 1 cup)
water
4 disposable plastic containers (2 cups or greater)
measuring spoon
1/3 cup of each: salt, borax, Epsom salts
3 tablespoons unscented household ammonia
food coloring

Procedure:

1. Place the charcoal in the bag. Use the hammer to break into small pieces. (Be sure to get permission to do this project and make sure the location is appropriate.)

2. If bluing is dry, mix powder with an equal amount of water. If bluing is liquid, add about 6 tablespoons of water to it.

3. In a separate container, mix 1/3 cup of bluing, 1/3 cup of water, and 1 tablespoon ammonia with the 1/3 cup of salt. Rinse the container before reusing.

4. Place 1/3 of the charcoal in a plastic container and pour the solution over it. Add a drop of food coloring on top of the charcoal. Label the container and put it somewhere safe and where it can sit undisturbed for a day.

5. Repeat steps 3 and 4 twice, using borax and Epson salts.

6. **Do not move the containers! The crystals will break easily.**

The crystals will form on the surface of the charcoal, which has absorbed some of the water. The other ingredients mix together to form the crystals. As the water is absorbed by the charcoal, small particles of the salts evaporate out of the water and bond in a repeating pattern. Millions of these small particles join together to form the crystal shapes. Notice that each type of chemical forms a crystal with a different shape.

On a separate piece of paper, draw and label each of the crystal structures. What observations can you make for each of them?

Pronoun and Antecedent. The *antecedent* of a pronoun is the word or group of words to which the pronoun refers. A pronoun must agree with its antecedent in number and gender. Write the antecedent for each underlined pronoun.

1. Carla did research for the report that <u>she</u> wrote. _____
2. Her report was about Sweden, and <u>it</u> was for school. _____
3. Carla used two libraries, and <u>they</u> had great information. _____
4. Sweden's wealth of natural resources has made <u>it</u> a prosperous country. _____
5. All of the sixth grade students brought <u>their</u> lunches to the school picnic. _____
6. Would you please lend me <u>one</u> of your coats? _____
7. The students turned in <u>their</u> research papers on time. _____
8. Dr. Harrison measured Keith's heartbeat. <u>It</u> was normal. _____
9. George won first place in the competition. <u>He</u> is a great athlete. _____
10. Sara and Juanita have made up <u>their</u> minds to do all their homework. _____

An *adjective* is a word that modifies, or describes, a noun or a pronoun. <u>Remember</u>: An adjective tells what kind, which one, or how many about something. Circle the adjective or adjectives in each sentence. Do not circle *a*, *an*, or *the*.

11. We stayed at Lake Hotel in Yellowstone National Park for several days.
12. Red, yellow, and blue balloons decorated the ballroom.
13. Kelly saw those priceless paintings in the museum in New York.
14. Providence is a historical city in Rhode Island.
15. The contest rules are on the back of the green folder.
16. Tony's sculptures, bright and unusual, are on display in the auditorium.
17. These science projects are the best I have seen in years.
18. Alice, quiet and studious, is always on time for class.
19. Ginger is a beautiful, clever dancer.
20. We have endured five days of hard, steady rain.

Rewrite each mixed number as a fraction. *Example:*

Step 1. Multiply the denominator by the whole number. $2\frac{3}{4}$ (2 × 4) = 8

Step 2. Add the numerator to the product.   3 + 8 = 11

Step 3. Write the sum over the denominator. $\frac{11}{4}$

1. $2\frac{1}{2}$ $\frac{5}{2}$

2. $4\frac{4}{5}$ $\frac{24}{5}$

3. $2\frac{3}{8}$ $\frac{19}{8}$

4. $4\frac{1}{5}$ $\frac{21}{5}$

5. $3\frac{2}{5}$ $\frac{17}{5}$

6. $2\frac{2}{3}$ $\frac{8}{3}$

7. $6\frac{1}{3}$ $\frac{19}{3}$

8. $6\frac{7}{9}$ $\frac{61}{9}$

Rewrite each fraction as a mixed or whole number. Use division to change fractions to a whole or mixed number.

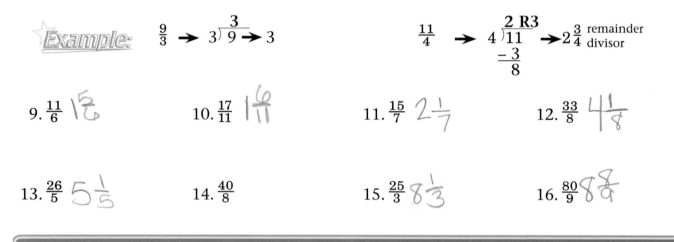

Example: $\frac{9}{3} \rightarrow 3\overline{)9} \rightarrow 3$

$\frac{11}{4} \rightarrow 4\overline{)11} \begin{array}{r} 2\,R3 \\ -\,\frac{3}{8} \end{array} \rightarrow 2\frac{3}{4}$ remainder divisor

9. $\frac{11}{6}$ $1\frac{5}{6}$

10. $\frac{17}{11}$ $1\frac{6}{11}$

11. $\frac{15}{7}$ $2\frac{1}{7}$

12. $\frac{33}{8}$ $4\frac{1}{8}$

13. $\frac{26}{5}$ $5\frac{1}{5}$

14. $\frac{40}{8}$

15. $\frac{25}{3}$ $8\frac{1}{3}$

16. $\frac{80}{9}$ $8\frac{8}{9}$

Write the quotient (answer) as a mixed number. Write the fraction in lowest terms.

17. $9\overline{)39}$ $4\frac{3}{9}$

18. $15\overline{)50}$

19. $8\overline{)38}$

20. $12\overline{)78}$

21. The school's snack bar is selling popcorn by the bag or box.
Each bag will fill half of a box.
How many boxes are needed to hold 6 bags of popcorn?

22. The average serving of potatoes is 6 oz.
How many servings are in 2 lb. of potatoes?

Central America, the isthmus stretching from Mexico to Columbia, contains seven independent nations. Label each country, and use a ★ to indicate each capital. Then label the capitals. You may need an atlas.

Central America

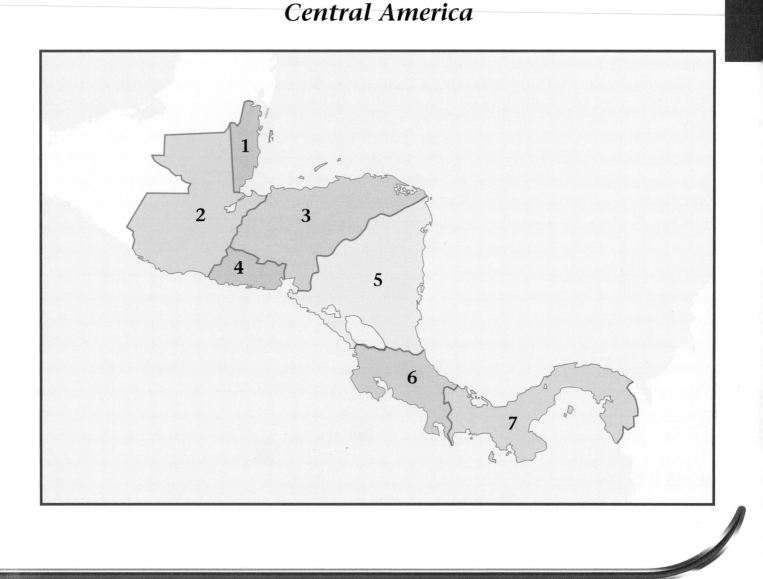

Create a Travel Brochure

Each of the Central American countries has an interesting history and culture as well as unique physical geography. Choose one of the seven countries you would like to learn more about and create a travel brochure for the country. Include the capital city and its interesting attractions, the country's scenery, plants, animals, culture, historical facts, and sights. Decorate your brochure with the country's flag and other appropriate symbols. The Internet home page for each country is an excellent source of information.

Earthquakes. The theory of continental drift says that the continents are drifting slowly around the earth. A companion theory is plate tectonics, which says that Earth's crust consists of various moving plates. When these massive continental plates collide or move past each other, at points known as fault lines, earthquakes occur. Earthquakes occur every 30 seconds somewhere in the world. That adds up to over one million quakes a year. Seismographs all over the world record this activity. They record the primary and secondary waves produced by the quake. The Richter scale measures the relative strength, or magnitude, of a quake: the higher the magnitude, the stronger the quake.

Earthquakes can cause everything from tsunamis (large waves often originating at the epicenter of an earthquake) to landslides caused by the upheaval of rocks and mud. Aftershocks are common after an earthquake. These often cause more damage than the main shock by collapsing structures weakened by the initial energy waves.

seismograph
earthquake
fault lines
tsunami
epicenter
landslide
aftershocks
Richter scale
continental
drift
plate tectonics
waves
magnitude

Across:

1. theory stating that present-day continents drifted to their present locations
3. the name given to a seismic sea wave
5. shaking of the ground
10. theory that Earth's surface is divided into plates that move
11. the downhill movement of rocks or mud
12. a scale that rates the strength, or magnitude, of an earthquake

Down:

2. the point directly above the focus of a quake
4. the instrument used to measure the strength of an earthquake
6. the secondary quakes following a main shock
7. a crack in the earth's crust where movement has occurred
8. relative strength of an earthquake
9. the form in which energy travels in an earthquake

A *conjunction* is a word that connects words or groups of words. Circle the coordinating, correlative, or subordinating conjunction(s) in each sentence.

1. I really enjoy watching television, but I cannot watch it too often.

2. Because my parents do not like to watch television, I often read or study.

3. Do you like to play football or basketball?

4. Either you do this report or you will not pass this course.

5. When my sister returned from the mall, she had spent over two hundred dollars.

6. Neither movies nor television can compare to a great book.

7. Susan opened her locker, and she found a note from her boyfriend.

8. Although Tony had finished all of his homework, he was not prepared for the quiz.

9. Angela finished writing the letter, but she did not mail it.

10. Yvonne has loved to dance since she was three.

Need Help?
Check Out
Grammar Links at
www.SummerBridgeActivities.com

Subjects and Verbs Agree. Circle the correct form of the verb for each sentence. Be sure to check your answer by reading the completed sentence to yourself.

11. At the state science fair, the winner (receives, receive) a trophy and a plaque.

12. The assistant principal (makes, make) the afternoon announcements each day.

13. To earn money, Denise and Donna (does, do) chores after school.

14. The principal said either pants or a skirt (is, are) appropriate at school.

15. You (was, were) the only one to finish the research paper on time.

16. The singer in the photographs (has, have) performed well all week long.

17. The dogs in the pet shop (looks, look) so cute and adorable.

18. In that closet (is, are) my old clothes, shoes, and coats.

19. The football players and their coach (practices, practice) every day.

20. California and Nevada (shares, share) a border.

Fractions to Decimals. To convert a fraction to a decimal, divide the numerator by the denominator. Zeros can be added after the decimal point in the dividend as often as needed until the digits in the quotient begin to repeat (repeating decimal). A repeating decimal may be shown by drawing a bar over the digit or digits that repeat. When the answer is a repeating decimal, it is often rounded off. Mixed numbers may be written as decimals. Divide the fractional part of the mixed number. Add the whole number and the decimal.

Example: $2\frac{4}{5} = 2 + \frac{4}{5} \rightarrow 5\overline{)4.0}^{\,0.8} \rightarrow 2 + 0.8 = 2.8$

Write as a decimal. Round to the nearest thousandth when necessary.

1. $\frac{2}{5}$

2. $\frac{9}{40}$

3. $\frac{7}{80}$

4. $\frac{5}{9}$

5. $\frac{7}{22}$

6. $4\frac{7}{100}$

7. $9\frac{1}{8}$

8. $4\frac{5}{8}$

9. $\frac{9}{50}$

10. $\frac{1}{40}$

11. $\frac{1}{3}$

12. $\frac{7}{12}$

13. $\frac{5}{13}$

14. $8\frac{67}{100}$

15. $1\frac{3}{8}$

16. $5\frac{17}{25}$

17. $\frac{1}{50}$

18. $\frac{3}{8}$

19. $\frac{29}{64}$

20. $\frac{1}{15}$

21. $\frac{568}{1000}$

22. $7\frac{87}{100}$

23. $7\frac{2}{5}$

24. $3\frac{10}{15}$

25. $\frac{3}{4}$

26. $\frac{16}{25}$

27. $\frac{37}{45}$

28. $\frac{5}{6}$

Time Out: Which costs more per pound, a prime rib that costs $31.35 and weighs 5 lb. or a small car that costs $6,492 and weighs 1,200 lb.? Write the steps you would take to answer this question.

Incentive Contract Calendar

Month _____

My parents and I decided that if I complete 20 days of
Summer Bridge Activities™ 6–7 and read _____ minutes a day,
my incentive/reward will be:

_____

Child's Signature_____

Parent's Signature_____

EXAMPLE: ☑ ☑ _AC_

Day 1 ☐ ☐ _____   Day 10 ☐ ☐ _____
Day 2 ☐ ☐ _____   Day 11 ☐ ☐ _____
Day 3 ☐ ☐ _____   Day 12 ☐ ☐ _____
Day 4 ☐ ☐ _____   Day 13 ☐ ☐ _____
Day 5 ☐ ☐ _____   Day 14 ☐ ☐ _____
Day 6 ☐ ☐ _____   Day 15 ☐ ☐ _____
Day 7 ☐ ☐ _____   Day 16 ☐ ☐ _____
Day 8 ☐ ☐ _____   Day 17 ☐ ☐ _____
Day 9 ☐ ☐ _____   Day 18 ☐ ☐ _____
                          Day 19 ☐ ☐ _____
                          Day 20 ☐ ☐ _____

Child: Put a ✔ in the ☐ for the daily activities completed.

Put a ✔ in the ☐ for the daily reading completed.

Parent: Initial the _____ for daily activities and reading your child completes.

Best Day/Vacation So Far

Write about It

Picture

Picture

Picture

Write about It

Caribbean Islands and Nations. Use the Word Bank below and an encyclopedia, atlas, or other reference materials to help fill in the blanks.

The many islands of the Caribbean are really partially submerged peaks of a mountain range. These "chains" of islands are called archipelagoes. The major island groups in this area are the (1)_____, the Greater and Lesser Antilles, the Leeward, and (2)__ _____ Islands. The significant bodies of water in the Caribbean are the Atlantic Ocean, the (3)_____, the Gulf of Mexico, and the Straits of Florida. The Tropic of Cancer is north of Cuba and runs through the (4)_____ and the Bahamas. The second largest island in the area is (5)_____; French-speaking Haiti and the Spanish-speaking Dominican Republic are independent nations located on it. Colonialism has left its mark throughout the (6)_____. Many of the smaller islands are still territories of the U.S. or (7)_____ powers. (8)_____, French, Spanish, and English languages and place names continue to show the impact of those who fol- lowed Columbus to the New World. A limited number of safe passages for ships through the islands make shipping lanes very predictable. (9)_____ is the name given to the shores of lands bordering the Caribbean. Caribbean nations are tiny by world stan- dards but have high population densities, especially in larger cities along the vast coast- lines. (10)_____ continues to be a problem as high birth rates and the disappear- ance of plantation agriculture prevent the development of a middle class.

Word Bank

Caribbean
Poverty
Bahamas Islands
Hispaniola
Caribbean Sea
Dutch
European
Rimland
Windward
Straits of Florida

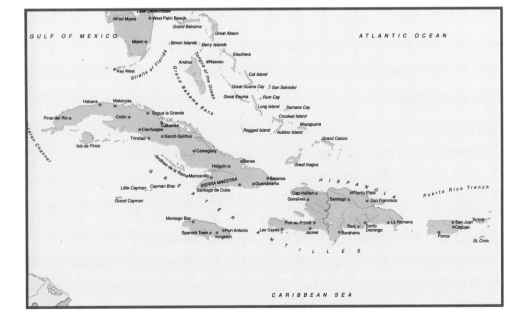

Chemical Reactions. A *mixture* is made when two or more materials are combined with no reaction—for example: mixing salt, sand, and sugar. A *solution* is created when one material dissolves in another with no reaction—for example: salt or sugar in warm water. A *reaction* occurs when two materials combine to form a new substance.

Materials:
clear plastic cups
water
white vinegar
baking soda
plastic spoons
paper towels

Procedure:

1. Place a cup on the paper towel and fill halfway with water.
2. Stir in several spoonfuls of baking soda. Stir continuously until the solution is clear.
3. Predict what will happen when vinegar is added.
4. Pour 1/4 cup of vinegar into the solution.
5. Draw what happened when the vinegar was added.

What's the Matter—Creating a Polymer

Materials:
borax
water
white glue
food coloring
plastic spoons
self-sealing plastic bag
paper towel

Procedure:

1. Dissolve 1/2 cup of borax in 1 quart of very hot water. Set aside to cool.
2. Place 2 spoonfuls of water in a plastic bag.
3. Add 3 spoonfuls of white glue.
4. Seal the bag; then, squish and squeeze to mix.
5. Open the bag and add 2 spoonfuls of borax solution. (Be sure to use a clean spoon.)
6. Seal the bag, making sure to push out all excess air.
7. Observe the changes that occur as you squish and squeeze the bag.
8. When totally thickened, remove the "gloop" and roll and stretch it.

South America. On the map below, label each country in South America and its corresponding capital. You may need an atlas.

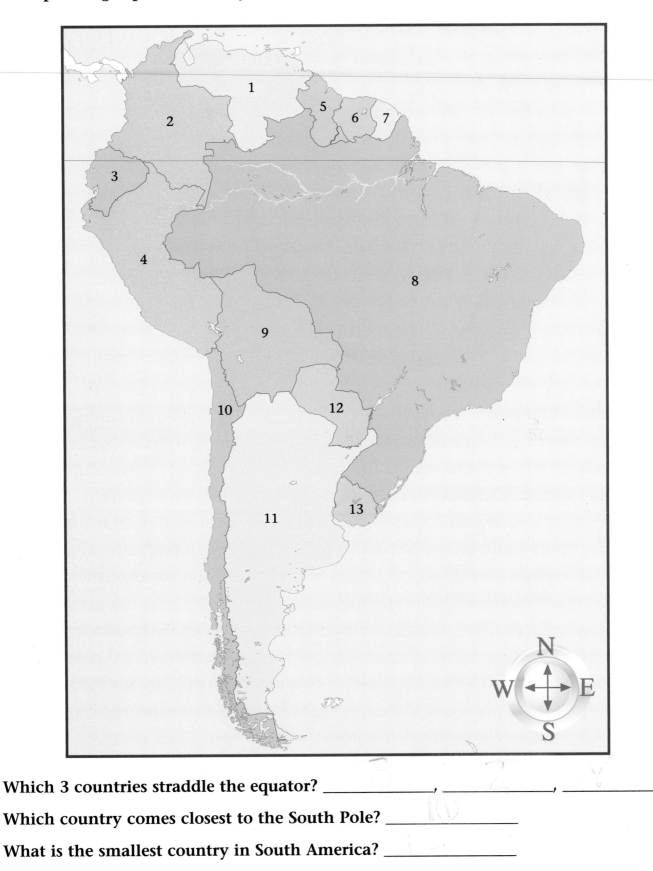

Which 3 countries straddle the equator? _____, _____, _____

Which country comes closest to the South Pole? _____

What is the smallest country in South America? _____

_____ is between Peru and Paraguay.

Layers of the Earth. Label each layer of the earth model below.

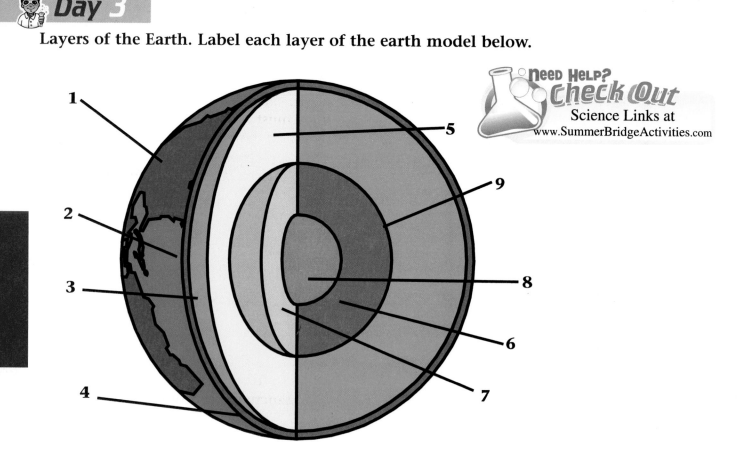

Need Help? Check Out Science Links at www.SummerBridgeActivities.com

The outside of the earth is called the (1)_____. The crust is the part of the earth that we see, live on, and explore. The (2)_____, or Moho, is the boundary that separates the crust from the top part of the mantle. The (3)_____ is the upper, solid layer of the earth including the crust and the cooler part of the upper mantle. The (4)_____ is about 1,802 miles thick and is composed of silica, iron, magnesium, and other minerals. Convection in this portion of the earth helps create the motion seen in plate tectonics. The (5)_____ is hot, semisolid, and approximately 186 miles thick. It is the layer below the lithosphere. The (6)_____ of the earth consists of the (7)_____ _____, which is about 1,400 miles thick and appears to be liquid, and the (8)_____ _____, which is approximately 800 miles thick and appears to be solid. It is very hot, with temperatures between 7,200 and 9,000 degrees Fahrenheit. The (9)_____ _____, named after the German geologist that discovered it, separates the earth's mantle from the outer core.

asthenosphere	Mohorovicic discontinuity	outer core
lithosphere	Gutenberg discontinuity	crust
core	mantle	inner core

Reading Comprehension. Read "Tiger Town." Then answer the questions that follow.

Yesterday, I read a story in the newspaper about a place in Montana called Tiger Town. Tiger Town is an animal sanctuary for large cats like tigers, lions, leopards, pumas, and jaguars. A sanctuary is a lot like a shelter for dogs or house cats, except it's permanent.

These sanctuaries are necessary because there are, surprisingly, a lot of homeless large cats. It's hard to imagine a homeless tiger, but many states have no licensing requirements or regulations for buying and keeping these great cats. Because of this, some people buy a tiger when it is a cub, only to find out later that they have a wild animal, not a pet, on their hands. Experts will tell you that there is simply no way to make a house pet out of a tiger, a lion, or any big cat. However, most owners do not discover this until it's too late.

For this and other reasons, big cats often find themselves without a home, and they must be placed somewhere or be destroyed. Sanctuaries are a humane option because they never sell the animals or breed them. They are safe places where the cats are fed a proper diet and given medical attention and wide-open spaces where they can relax and be content for as long as they live.

Because of a lack of funding and trained personnel, there aren't many animal sanctuaries like these in the United States. It is estimated that there are over 5,000 big cats in private ownership across the country. As more states pass legislation banning possession of big cats, the need for sanctuaries grows.

The sanctuary in Montana takes donations. I've decided to send in some of the money I've accumulated in my savings account. I want to help in any way I can!

Questions on "Tiger Town"

1. Tiger Town is located in
   A. southern Oregon.   B. Montana.   C. northern Utah.   D. Las Vegas.

2. The story is mainly about
   A. what great pets tigers make.   C. the importance of animal sanctuaries.
   B. the slow extinction of tigers.   D. saving your money.

3. To pass legislation is to
   A. enact a law.   C. take away someone's license.
   B. convict a criminal.   D. punish tiger owners.

4. How many cats are estimated to be in private ownership across the country?
   A. 500   B. 3   C. 6,000   D. 5,000

5. A synonym for **humane** is
   A. clean.   B. compassionate.   C. orderly.   D. professional.

6. What makes an animal sanctuary different from an animal shelter?
   A. It's larger.   B. It's temporary.   C. It's permanent.   D. It's not different.

7. Which of the following is not the kind of cat housed at an animal sanctuary?
   A. Siamese   B. tiger   C. leopard   D. puma

8. The sanctuaries need donations because
   A. they lack funding & trained personnel.   C. they don't spend their money wisely.
   B. large cats like to receive gifts.   D. they don't need donations.

Adding and Subtracting Mixed Numbers. To add a mixed number, first rewrite all of the fractions with a common denominator. Then add the fractions. Add the whole numbers and simplify the answers.

Example:
$$5 \tfrac{2}{3} \qquad 5 \tfrac{8}{12}$$
$$+ 4 \tfrac{3}{4} \qquad + 4 \tfrac{9}{12}$$
$$\overline{\qquad\qquad 9 \tfrac{17}{12}} \; = \; 9 + 1 \tfrac{5}{12} = 10 \tfrac{5}{12}$$

To subtract fractions or mixed numbers with unlike denominators, rewrite fractions as equivalent fractions with a common denominator. Subtract the fractions. Subtract the whole numbers.

Example:
$$6 \tfrac{5}{6} \qquad\qquad 6 \tfrac{5}{6}$$
$$- 4 \tfrac{1}{3} \;\; = \;\; - 4 \tfrac{2}{6}$$
$$\overline{\qquad\qquad 2 \tfrac{3}{6} = 2 \tfrac{1}{2}}$$

1.
$$3 \tfrac{9}{10}$$
$$+ \;\; 4 \tfrac{1}{4}$$

2.
$$12 \tfrac{3}{4}$$
$$- \;\; 4 \tfrac{7}{20}$$

3.
$$7 \tfrac{5}{12}$$
$$- \;\; 3 \tfrac{1}{6}$$

4.
$$6 \tfrac{7}{8}$$
$$+ \;\; 4 \tfrac{1}{4}$$

5.
$$3 \tfrac{9}{10}$$
$$+ \;\; 4 \tfrac{7}{10}$$

6.
$$9 \tfrac{5}{12}$$
$$- \;\; 7 \tfrac{1}{16}$$

7.
$$11 \tfrac{2}{3}$$
$$- \;\; 7 \tfrac{3}{5}$$

8.
$$8 \tfrac{1}{2}$$
$$+ \;\; 7 \tfrac{3}{5}$$

9.
$$15 \tfrac{2}{3}$$
$$- \;\; 8 \tfrac{3}{8}$$

Africa from A to Z. For each letter of the alphabet, identify at least one physical or political feature on the continent of Africa.

NEED HELP? CHECK OUT Social Science Links at www.SummerBridgeActivities.com

Materials: Maps of Africa, an atlas, or the Internet

A is for _african_

B is for _breakfast-barrito_

C is for _culture_

D is for _dance_

E is for _eggs_

F is for _feast_

G is for _great food_

H is for _holidays_

I is for _isolated_

J is for _amaican_

K is for _koalas_

L is for _ima beans_

M is for _mauntains_

N is for _Nocternal_

O is for _opisites_

P is for _Poor_

Q is for _quit popular_

R is for _religion_

S is for _stars_

T is for _tortilla_

U is for _universe_

V is for _Virtues_

W is for _women_

X is for _X-rays_

Y is for _____

Z is for _zoo animals_

A F R I C A

Static Electricity. The English word *electricity* comes from the Greek word for amber, *elecktron*. Ancient Greeks discovered that when a piece of fur was rubbed over a chunk of amber, the amber would pick up straw, hair, and various other fine, lightweight items. Rubbing stocking feet across a carpet and then touching someone or something like a doorknob will release a static charge. Things with the same charge push away from each other, while things with opposite charges attract each other.

Materials:
tissue paper torn in tiny pieces

several pieces of cloth (i.e., wool, felt, nylon, or silk)

a collection of small "stuff" (i.e., nail, comb, paper clip, glass chip, etc.)

Procedure:

1. Choose one object and one cloth scrap. Rub the object vigorously with the cloth.

2. Hold the object close to the tissue paper. If the object attracts the tissue paper, it has been charged with static electricity. Record your results on a blank sheet of paper.

3. Repeat with the same object and a different piece of cloth. Record each result. Be sure to wipe the object with your hand after each trial. Test to make sure this has removed the static charge before beginning the new trial.

4. Repeat for each object with each fabric scrap. *Hint*: Some items may need to be warmed in your hands before they will accept the charge.

5. After all trials have been completed, decide which types of substances are easiest to charge with static electricity.

Note: This experiment will work best in a cool, dry environment.

Magic Rabbits. Did you know that you can use rabbits to show the magic of static electricity? No, you won't pull them out of a hat, but you can make them jump at your command!

Now, try this:
Lay two thick books several inches apart on a table. Rest a sheet of glass from a picture frame on the books. Cut out some tiny paper rabbits and put them on the table under the glass. Now, really concentrate on the rabbits. Then mumble a few magic words to impress your spectators. Rub the glass with some silk or flannel. Bingo! The rabbits come alive!

Here's how it is done:
When you rub the glass, you give it a static charge. The glass attracts the rabbits. They pick up the same charge while they stick to the glass, so they are pushed away by the glass; therefore, they jump back down.

Western Europe and Scandinavia. Use the numbers from the map below or names of countries to answer the following questions. You may need an atlas.

1. Where is France? _____
2. Number 12, one the smallest countries in Europe, is _____.
3. Where is Denmark? _____
4. Is # 20 Sweden, Norway, or Finland? _____
5. Where is Portugal? _____
6. Where is Wales? _____

7. Where would you go to visit the prince of Monaco? _____
8. Where would you find the city of Rome? _____
9. Where is the country famous for tulips, windmills, and wooden shoes? _____
10. Germany, Austria, and Italy all share borders with this mountainous country. _____

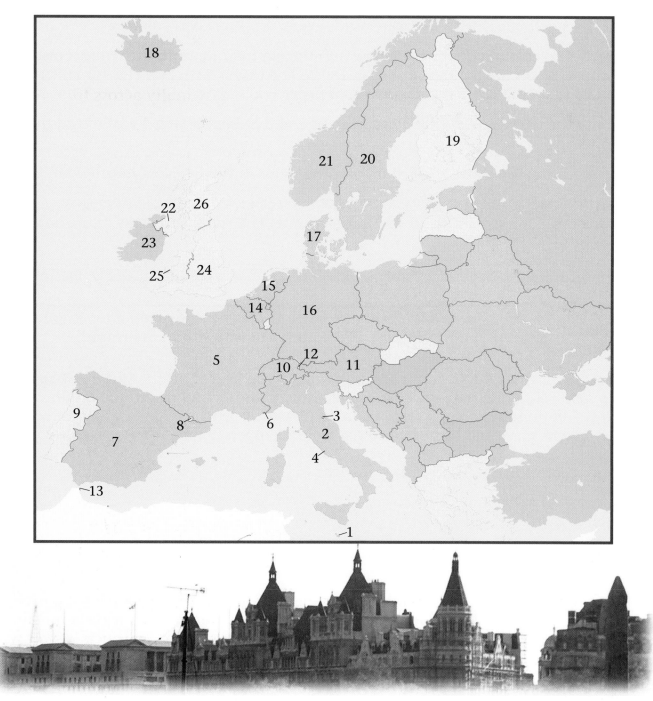

 **Day 7**

Heat Flow. Look at the pavement on a hot summer day. Shimmering just above the ground the hot air can be seen rising from the hot ground. A desert mirage is actually an example of this heat flow.

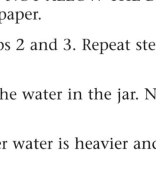

Materials:

large jar   food coloring
small bottle   cold water
string   hot water

Procedure:

1. Tie a string around the neck of the bottle.

2. Fill a large jar with cold water.

3. Fill the small bottle with hot water and several drops of food coloring.

4. Slowly and carefully lower the bottle into the jar, holding onto the string. Lower the bottle to sit on the bottom of the jar. DO NOT ALLOW THE BOTTLE TO TIP OVER. Record the results on a separate sheet of paper.

5. Empty the bottle and the jar. Reverse steps 2 and 3. Repeat step 4 and record the results.

6. Try repeating the above steps, but color the water in the jar. Now record your results.

As water is heated, it expands and rises. Cooler water is heavier and sinks to the bottom.

Did You Know? A glass of hot water looks fairly innocent; however, a lot is going on inside it. Add just a pinch of sawdust and watch the way it moves around.

Next, put the sawdust into a glass container that can be heated on the stove. ***Ask an adult to help you.*** Watch the sawdust as the water heats up, and record the results. As water at the bottom heats up, it rises, taking the sawdust with it. Cooler water moves down to take its place and be heated. What would happen if a microwave oven were used?

Try it and record the results. Compare the two.

A wood, rubber, or metal spoon? Why do you stir soup on the stove with a rubber or wooden spoon? If you leave a metal spoon in the pot for a few minutes and then touch it, you will know why! (Caution! Don't try this!) So we can easily see that some things pick up heat much faster than others.

Direct and Indirect Objects. A *direct object* is a noun or pronoun in the predicate that receives the action of the verb. To find the direct object, ask *who?* or *what?* after the action verb. An *indirect object* is a noun or pronoun in the predicate that answers the question *whom? for whom? to what?* or *for what?* after an action verb. Circle the verb in each sentence. Correctly label whether the underlined word is a direct object (DO) or indirect object (IO) on the line provided.

1. On the fourth of July we ate barbecued <u>chicken</u>. _____
2. Sarah's mother offered the <u>guests</u> a piece of pie. _____
3. Mrs. L wrote the <u>assignment</u> on the blackboard. _____
4. Michelle bought her <u>pet</u> a new toy. _____
5. Farmer n fed his <u>horses</u> all the corn. _____
6. The speaker gave that <u>question</u> some thought before answering. _____
7. My uncle told my little brother a ghost <u>story</u>. _____
8. The front desk clerk gave my mother and me <u>directions</u>. _____
9. Mr. Pow feeds his <u>birds</u> food once a day. _____
10. The salesman sold us the last school <u>sweatshirt</u>. _____

Identifying Parts of Speech—Review. Identify the part of speech of the underlined word in each sentence by placing a number in the blank provided: 1-*noun*; 2-*pronoun*; 3-*verb*; 4-*adjective*; 5-*adverb*; 6-*preposition*; 7-*conjunction*; 8-*interjection*.

_____ 11. <u>We</u> looked everywhere for Mother's rings.
_____ 12. <u>Look</u>! You are too close to the cliff's edge.
_____ 13. Aunt gathered all the ingredients before baking the cake.
_____ 14. The bomb exploded so <u>quickly</u> that we could not believe it.
_____ 15. My father said that the chocolate <u>cake</u> was delicious.
_____ 16. We visit Denver <u>because</u> my mother has relatives there.
_____ 17. Orlando, Florida, is a very <u>popular</u> tourist attraction.
_____ 18. Franklin poured a bucket of water <u>over</u> the smoldering campfire.
_____ 19. The last number on the <u>program</u> was an overture by Wagner.
_____ 20. <u>Without</u> a word of protest, the teacher sealed the letter.
_____ 21. The lemonade <u>tasted</u> very sour.
_____ 22. From that corner <u>she</u> could see my face.
_____ 23. On her pantry shelves were spread jars of canned apples, pears, <u>and</u> peaches.
_____ 24. My grandfather noticed <u>an</u> old ladder standing against the stone wall.

Day 8

Multiplying Mixed Numbers. First, write the mixed number as an improper fraction. Whole numbers may be written with a denominator of 1. Simplify your answer.

$$5\frac{2}{3} \times 12 = \frac{17}{3} \times \frac{12}{1} = \frac{204}{3} = \frac{68}{1} = 68$$

To multiply two mixed numbers, first write both mixed numbers as improper fractions.

$$2\frac{2}{7} \times 4\frac{1}{4} = \frac{16}{7} \times \frac{17}{4} = \frac{68}{7} = 9\frac{5}{7}$$

Solve the problems below.

1. $4\frac{2}{3} \times 2\frac{5}{8}$

2. $3\frac{7}{8} \times 4$

3. $7\frac{5}{8} \times 2\frac{1}{3}$

4. $3\frac{1}{7} \times 5\frac{1}{12}$

5. $6\frac{4}{12} \times 3$

6. $2\frac{3}{5} \times 4$

Reciprocals are a pair of numbers whose product is 1.

$$\frac{5}{6} \times \frac{6}{5} = 1 \qquad\qquad \frac{8}{7} \times \frac{7}{8} = 1 \qquad\qquad \frac{3}{1} \times \frac{1}{3} = 1$$

The product of 0 and any number is always 0, never 1. Zero has no reciprocal.

Write the reciprocal.

7. $\frac{3}{5}$ $\frac{5}{3} = \frac{15}{15} = 1$

8. $\frac{4}{8}$

9. $\frac{7}{11}$

10. $\frac{6}{12}$

11. $\frac{5}{9}$

12. $\frac{3}{4}$

13. 8

14. $\frac{8}{11}$

15. $\frac{18}{21}$

16. 25

17. 142

18. $\frac{4}{7}$

19. $\frac{13}{14}$

20. $\frac{6}{25}$

21. 32

22. 16

Eastern Europe. The European continent is divided both physically and culturally into Eastern and Western Europe. Since the breakup of the USSR, the countries of Eastern Europe have been expanded to include several countries in northern Asia. Use the numbers from the map below to answer the following questions. You may need an atlas.

Moscow is located here. ___

This country sounds like it hasn't eaten in a while. ___

This country sounds like a tasty Thanksgiving dinner. ___

This country is bordered by Poland to the west and Ukraine to the south. ___

This country is sandwiched between Lithuania and Estonia. ___

Prague is the capital of this republic. ___

This country borders both Turkey and the Black Sea. ___

Sarajevo, home to the 1984 Winter Olympics, is found here. ___

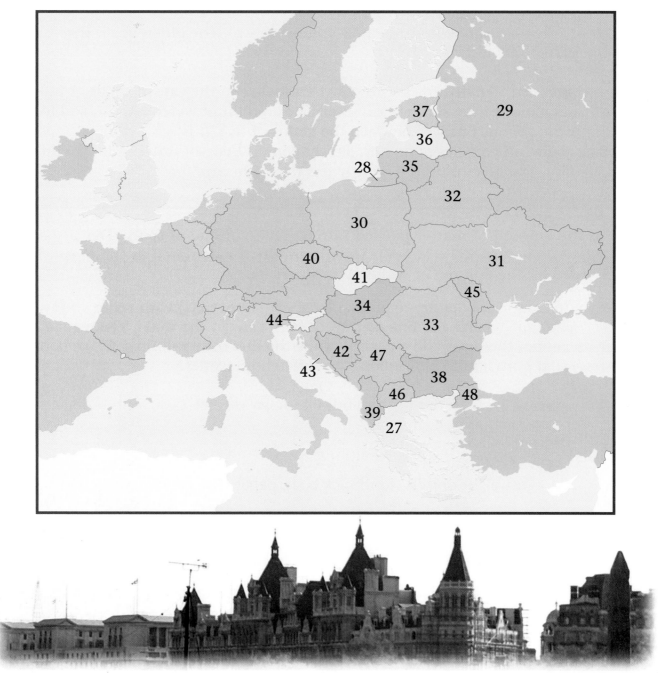

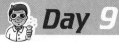

Volume is the amount of space something occupies. The mathematical formula for expressing volume is length times width times height (V = L × W × H). Some objects allow for increase and decrease of volume; for example, a balloon that expands or deflates. Water displacement is a method for measuring the volume of a solid.

Materials: measuring cup or beaker, with measurements indicated
water
small, heavy object (a small rock works well)

Procedure:

1. Fill the beaker about half full of water; record the volume (amount) of water (value a).
2. Predict the volume of the object.
3. Sink the object in the cup until it is totally submerged. Measure the volume of water plus the object together (value b).
4. Subtract original volume from the new volume (b – a). The difference is the volume of the solid object.

Space exists between all particles. This is easy to visualize in the case of solids. A full cup of rice will still allow for the addition of water. The amount of water you can add to the cup of rice is the volume of space between the grains of rice. It is more difficult to visualize the space between particles of liquids. Slowly pour 1/2 cup of water into 1/2 cup of rubbing alcohol. The new volume is slightly less than one cup.

Density is the amount of matter packed into a given volume of space. Density equals mass divided by volume (D = M ÷ V). *Specific gravity* is calculated as the mass of an object divided by the volume of water it displaces.

A good demonstration for density requires a large container filled with water and two 12 oz. cans of soda, one regular and one diet. Place both cans in the water. The regular soda is denser because of the sugar and will sink, while the diet soda will float. Wave bottles demonstrate that both liquids and solids have different densities.

Materials: clear jar with tight-fitting lid (plastic jar is fine)
mineral or vegetable oil
water
food coloring
lightweight objects (toothpick boat, paper clip, small plastic charm)

Procedure:

1. Clean the jar; be sure to remove all labels.
2. Fill the jar about half full of oil.
3. Add water and a few drops of food coloring to fill the jar.
4. Add objects, tighten cap, and tip the jar.
5. Slowly move the jar back and forth on its side; observe the wave action.
6. Record your observations about density.

need Help? Check Out
Science Links at
www.SummerBridgeActivities.com

Professional baseball players earn large salaries. Of course, they earn more than our police officers, firefighters, or even office workers. Naturally, they work shorter hours and for only part of a year. Many people think that baseball players earn too much for just playing ball. Others think that baseball players should earn as much as television and movie stars. Write a paragraph in which you state whether baseball players are paid too much or not. Explain your point of view. If you need additional space, use another sheet of paper.

_____

_____

_____

_____

_____

_____

_____

_____

_____

_____

_____

_____

Proofread this friendly letter. Correct any errors in spelling, capitalization, punctuation, or language usage.

aug 10 2000

Dear aunt Emily and uncle Bob;

Thank you so much for my Twelfieth birthday party. All of my friends really enjoyed the pizza and skating Party at Sals skating Palace.

Mom and dad must have tell you that i wanted a pizza and Skating party, i have hear from almost everyone who attended. What a great time?

As soon as the pictures is developed, me and Mom will send you some of the prints. I cant waite to see them!

Thanks again for such a wunderful birthday party.

Love,

Marsha

Dividing Fractions and Whole Numbers. To divide a fraction by a whole number, convert the whole number to an improper fraction and multiply by the reciprocal of the divisor.

$$\frac{3}{4} \div 3 = \frac{3}{4} \div \frac{3}{1} = \frac{3}{4} \times \frac{1}{3} = \frac{3}{12} = \frac{1}{4}$$

Dividing Fractions. To divide by a fraction, multiply by the reciprocal of the divisor. To divide by $\frac{3}{8}$, multiply by its reciprocal, $\frac{8}{3}$.

$$\frac{3}{4} \div \frac{3}{8} = \frac{3}{4} \times \frac{8}{3} = \frac{24}{12} = \frac{2}{1} = 2$$

Dividing Mixed Numbers. First, convert mixed numbers to improper fractions; then multiply by the reciprocal of the divisor.

$$10 \div 1\frac{1}{4} = 10 \div \frac{5}{4} = 10 \times \frac{4}{5} = \frac{10}{1} \times \frac{4}{5} = \frac{40}{5} = \frac{8}{1} = 8$$

Solve the problems below.

1. $\frac{3}{4} \div \frac{1}{2}$

2. $\frac{5}{6} \div \frac{7}{12}$

3. $7 \div 1\frac{1}{8}$

4. $\frac{3}{4} \div \frac{2}{3}$

5. $6 \div 9\frac{1}{2}$

6. $11 \div 6\frac{7}{8}$

7. $\frac{5}{8} \div \frac{2}{3}$

8. $\frac{4}{11} \div \frac{12}{22}$

9. $8\frac{1}{3} \div 6\frac{1}{4}$

10. $17\frac{1}{8} \div 16\frac{1}{3}$

11. $\frac{1}{8} \div \frac{5}{6}$

12. $\frac{3}{10} \div \frac{2}{5}$

Write < , > , or = to compare the numbers.

13. $4\frac{1}{8} \div 2\frac{1}{3} \ \square \ 6\frac{1}{5} \div 1\frac{1}{2}$

14. $3\frac{1}{2} + 2\frac{1}{8} \ \square \ 4\frac{2}{3} - 1\frac{7}{8}$

15. $5\frac{1}{4} \times 2\frac{3}{8} \ \square \ 7\frac{1}{3} + 2\frac{1}{4}$

16. $15\frac{1}{2} \div 2\frac{3}{7} \ \square \ 14\frac{2}{3} \times 3\frac{1}{2}$

Ancient Greece. The people of ancient Greece had many gods and goddesses, including gods of music, war, and wisdom. The Greeks also created many myths about their gods to explain things that happened in the real world. These myths became the basis for Greek religion, poetry, music, art, and theater. Use the word list of gods and goddesses below to complete the ancient Greece crossword puzzle.

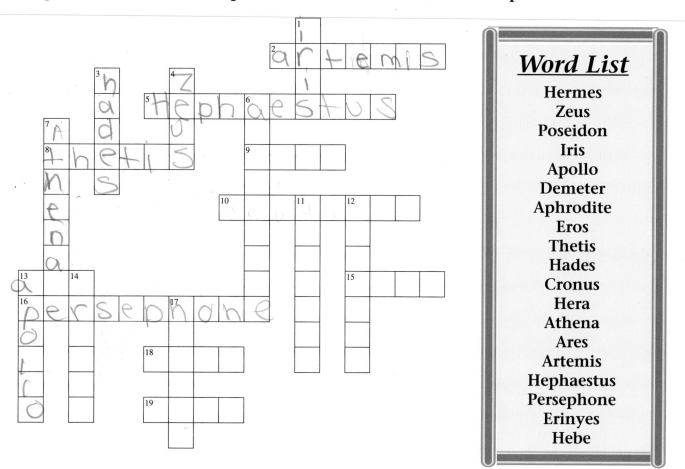

Word List

Hermes
Zeus
Poseidon
Iris
Apollo
Demeter
Aphrodite
Eros
Thetis
Hades
Cronus
Hera
Athena
Ares
Artemis
Hephaestus
Persephone
Erinyes
Hebe

Clues

Across

2. Goddess of hunting
5. God of fire
8. Mother of Achilles
9. Goddess of motherhood
10. God of the sea
15. God of love
16. Queen of the underworld
18. God of war
19. Goddess of youth

Down

1. Goddess of the rainbow
3. God of the dead
4. Supreme ruler of the gods
6. Goddess of beauty and love
7. Goddess of wisdom
11. Avengers of evil doing
12. Goddess of agriculture
13. God of poetry, music, and prophecy
14. Father of Zeus
17. Messenger of the gods

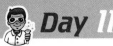
Facts about Plants. Plants grow from different beginnings—seeds, cuttings, tubers, or bulbs—but all follow a definite pattern of growth. Baby plants will grow to be like adult plants. Plants have different needs for temperature, sunshine, water, and soil. Try your own sprouting garden.

 **Materials:**

collection of seeds and cuttings from the kitchen and around your house

various containers for planting (egg cartons, old flower pots)

potting soil

sand

tiny pieces of charcoal (no lighter fluid)

vermiculite

water spritzer/spray bottle

humus

Procedure:

1. Citrus seeds—soak seeds overnight; mix sand and potting soil. You may use a fruit shell for initial sprouting or use other small "pots." Place layer of potting mixture in pot, add seeds, and cover with 1/2 inch of potting mixture. Spray each day with water; water well twice a week. Transfer young plant to a sturdier container.

2. Root vegetable tops—carrot, beet, turnip. Cut, retaining 1 inch of foliage and 1 inch of the root. Plant in sandy soil and keep moist, not wet. Alternative: set in a shallow pan of water (about 1/2 inch); add tiny pieces of charcoal to keep water sweet.

3. Irish potato, sweet potato, or yam—make sure potato is fresh, not heat dried. Look for sweet potatoes with a few whiskers. Cut potato in half. Insert toothpicks around the circumference of potato just above the cut (may be left whole with toothpicks inserted around the center). Suspend tapered end down in a jar by toothpicks. Fill jar with water. Place in a dark area until roots sprout. Then move into light. Keep water level constant. Plant may be left in water or transplanted into soil, allowing green sprouts to remain above the soil. Alternatives: Add food color to water; choose a yam with purple eyes. Cut a white potato in sections, each with an eye or two; plant in rich earth and keep moist (needs lots of light). Potato Porcupine: slice off top of an Irish potato and carve out a hole, leaving plenty of meat for side walls. Insert 4 toothpicks to serve as legs. Attach eyes (small white paper circles held in place with tacks). Fill cavity with soil and sprinkle with chives, grass, or other spiky seeds. Water often; it will sprout in about 10 days.

4. Seeds—birdseed, pepper, pumpkin, squash, melon. Punch small holes in bottom of a container for drainage. Fill container with soil and sprinkle seeds on soil. Cover with 1/4 inch of soil. Keep soil moist.

5. Beans, peas, lentils—Method 1: Spread in a single layer on a saucer; moisten but do not float seeds. Keep moist and in the sun. Seeds will sprout in about 10 days. Method 2: Soak 2–3 hours until beans swell. Roll drawing paper or other heavy weight paper into a tube and line a 1-pound, clear glass jar. Trim the paper at the mouth of the jar. Place the soaked beans 1/2 inch down between the jar and the paper. Pour 1 inch of water into the jar. Keep the paper wet. Put in a dark place to germinate. Then, bring into the light. Lay sprouted beans on the soil. Keep moist.

6. Pineapple tops, avocado and other pits, apple and other fruit seeds. Experiment to see what you can grow.

Combining Sentences. Good writers usually use some short sentences; however, they do not use them all the time. Combine each group of short, related sentences into one sentence by inserting adjectives, adverbs, or prepositional phrases. There may be more than one correct way to combine the sentences. Add commas where they are necessary.

1. Jennifer wrote her letter.
   She wrote it on Friday.
   It was a letter to the President.

   Jennifer wrote a letter to the President Friday

2. Joan finished the short story.
   Joan finally finished it.
   It was terribly boring.

   Joan finally finished the short story, but it was boring

3. The football players have arrived.
   They are ready to play.
   They are the varsity team.

   The varsity football team arived and
   is ready 2 play

4. During the summer I had a part-time job.
   I taught swimming at the club.
   The job was enjoyable.

   _____

5. We visited the zoo near my house.
   We went to see the elephants.
   We saw the giraffes.

   _____

6. We played softball in our backyard.
   We had a picnic.
   It was a beautiful day.

   _____

7. Rob did his assignment in class.
   The assignment was written.
   The class was math.

   _____

Day 12

Problem Solving—Fractions

1. Tanner has a picture that is 15 inches square. He wants to frame it using wood trim that is sold by the yard. How much trim will he need?

First, find the perimeter of the picture.	(p = 15" × 4 = 60")
Then, change inches to yards.	(y = 36")
Finally, reduce to the lowest terms.	(p ÷ 36)

2. Denise is making a bead necklace. The project calls for 72 white beads and 36 red beads. Beads cost 25¢ per dozen. What will the beads cost?

3. Deborah has created a wall hanging 22" × 38". What will it cost for edging to trim the picture if edging costs 39¢ per foot?

4. Grayson has a 12-gallon gasoline tank in his car. The gauge is registering $\frac{1}{8}$ full. Grayson knows he will burn $3\frac{1}{2}$ gallons of gas going to and from school.
   A. How much gas does he have now? _____
   B. Can Grayson make it to school and back today without buying gas? _____
   C. What is the least amount of gas Grayson can buy and not run out of gas before he gets home? _____
   D. How many gallons of gas would Grayson need to buy if he were to fill up now? _____

5. At Washington Middle School, $\frac{2}{3}$ of the sixth grade students like pizza. Five-eighths of these students also enjoy nachos. What fraction of the sixth graders will eat both pizza and nachos?

6. About $\frac{1}{6}$ of the sixth graders study French. Of these, $\frac{3}{4}$ are first-year students. What part of the students in the sixth grade are first-year French students?

The Roman Timeline. Latium, on the west coast of Italy, was the site of a group of villages near an island in the Tiber River. This location was chosen because it was a convenient place to cross the Tiber River. Here, according to legend, in 753 B.C., Rome was founded by Romulus after he killed his twin brother, Remus. Romulus became Rome's first king. Kings ruled Rome until 510 B.C. Rome then became a republic, governed by a group of citizens, the Senate. The city was defended by a wall and a strong army.

The Roman soldier is a true symbol of the Roman Empire. The soldier below guards a timeline of ancient Roman history. Match the events below with the correct dates by writing the corresponding letter in the blank beside the date given. Use reference books to help you with this timeline.

EVENTS

A. March 15 (Ides of March). Julius Caesar is murdered.

B. Trajan is emperor.

C. Hannibal crosses the Alps.

D. Throne auctioned to Didius Julianus, who is later murdered.

E. The First Triumvirate rules.

F. Christianity becomes official religion of Rome.

G. Reign of Augustus, the first Roman emperor.

H. Rome occupies Sicily, Corsica, and Sardinia.

I. Antoninus Pius is emperor. Rome's power is at its peak.

J. Rome captures Spain.

K. Diocletian divides empire into eastern and western halves.

L. Hadrian is emperor.

M. Carthage is captured.

N. Reign of Emperor Constantine, who reunites the empire.

DATES

_____ 241 B.C.

_____ 218 B.C.

_____ 206 B.C.

_____ 202 B.C.

_____ 60 B.C.

_____ 44 B.C.

_____ 31 B.C.–A.D. 14

_____ A.D. 98–117

_____ A.D. 117–138

_____ A.D. 138–161

_____ A.D. 193

_____ A.D. 293

_____ A.D. 306–337

_____ A.D. 313

NeeD HeLP? Check Out Social Science Links at www.SummerBridgeActivities.com

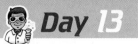
Day 13

Capillary Action—the process by which water travels up the stems to the leaves and flows through the veins (vascular bundles) in the stem of the plant. You can see it for yourself in this experiment.

Materials:
celery stalks with leaves and/or white flowers
      (daisy, carnation, or chrysanthemum)
food coloring (red or blue)
2 clear glass containers (drinking glasses or jars)
water
knife

Procedure:

1. Fill each glass with water. Then add 8–10 drops of food coloring to one glass.
2. Slice about 1/2 inch from the bottom of each stalk or stem. Carefully slit the bottom of each stalk or stem.
3. Place the bottom of one celery stalk and/or flower stem in the glass of clear water and another in the colored water. Record your observations about the stalk or stem, leaves, and flowers.
4. Set the experiment aside overnight.
5. Record your observations about the stalk and/or stem, leaves, and flowers.
6. Cut a 1-inch piece from the bottom of the stalk or stem. Draw what you observe. The colored dots are the vascular bundles that go up the stem.
7. Repeat the experiment using different flowers. Are the patterns of the vascular bundles in the stems the same or different?

Note: The stems of monocots and dicots are different. Vascular bundles of dicots are arranged in a circle. The vascular bundles of monocots are arranged in a more complex pattern.

Time Travel. Albert Einstein theorized that if the rate of travel is accelerated, time slows down. Some scientists think that it could be possible to accelerate to a point that would make time go in reverse. Science fiction writers use this theory when they suggest the possibility of time travel either backward or forward. This theory of time travel requires traveling faster than the speed of light. Light travels at about 186,000 miles per second. Is it possible to travel this fast? What would a time machine look like? Where in time would you travel? What adventure would await you?

Write a story about time travel; then draw and label a time machine. Use a separate sheet of paper. Use this space to brainstorm.

_____

_____

_____

_____

_____

© **Summer Bridge Activities™** 6–7   60   www.SummerBridgeActivities.com

Reviewing Comparative and Superlative. Use the *comparative* form of an adjective or adverb to compare two things, persons, places, or actions. The *superlative* form compares more than two things, persons, places, or actions. When you add *-er* or *-est* to form the comparative or superlative, the spelling of an adjective may change. Add *-er* or *-est* to all adverbs with one syllable and to some adverbs with two syllables. Use *more* or *most* with most adjectives and adverbs with two syllables and with all adverbs with more than one syllable. Do *not* combine *more* or *most* with *-er* or *-est*.

Complete the chart below with each form of the adjective or adverb.

Positive	Comparative	Superlative	Positive	Comparative	Superlative
1. happy			6. slowly		
2. beautiful			7. far		
3. weak			8. quietly		
4. talented			9. politely		
5. loud			10. high		

In each sentence, circle the correct form of the adjective or adverb in parentheses.

11. *Friends* is the (funnier, funniest) show of this television season.
12. The movie credits were (extreme, extremely) long.
13. Cindy read the story (more carefully, most carefully) than her younger sister did.
14. Martha was (sure, surely) she could finish her report on time.
15. She had done a (good, well) job of writing the paper.
16. Karen had prepared her speech (better, more better) than Philip.
17. Mrs. Clark listened to Karen (more attentively, most attentively) than I did.
18. Tomorrow will be (warmer, more warmer) than today.
19. A new swimsuit will be (expensiver, more expensive) than I expected.
20. Between Alicia and Marcia, Marcia is the (taller, tallest).
21. *Bridge to Teribithia* is the (greater, greatest) book I have ever read.
22. Which state is (bigger, biggest), California or Florida?
23. Marshall is the (faster, fastest) runner on the track team.
24. Who is the (most old, oldest) member in your family?
25. George is the (less, least) noisy person in this classroom.

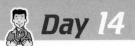

Ratios. A ratio, which is a quotient of two numbers, is used to compare one quantity to another. Ratios can be written in several ways but are usually read the same way. When a ratio is written as a fraction, it may be reduced to the lowest terms. Ratios are often written like this: 4 : 5. Usually we read this as 4 to 5.

★ ★ ★   🔔 🔔 🔔
★ ★ ★   🔔 🔔 🔔   6 stars   or 2 : 3
         🔔 🔔 🔔   9 bells

Ratio Problems. Write a ratio as a fraction in the lowest terms to compare numbers in a table.

Example:
Excellent to good 37 : 167 or $\frac{37}{167}$

1. fair to good   4. poor to fair

2. poor to excellent   5. excellent to total

3. good to fair   6. poor to total

Opinion	No. of Responses
Excellent	37
Good	167
Fair	154
Poor	58
TOTAL	416

Towers Middle School has 825 students and 43 teachers. Write the ratio as a fraction in lowest terms.

7. What is the ratio of students to teachers?

8. What is the ratio of teachers to students?

Sometimes ratios compare measurements. When they do, be certain the measurements are written in the same units. Rewrite the ratio so that both terms are expressed in the same unit. If possible, write the ratio in the lowest terms.

Example: $\frac{3 \text{ cm}}{1 \text{ m}} = \frac{3 \text{ cm}}{100 \text{ cm}} = \frac{3}{100}$

9. $\frac{12 \text{ minutes}}{1 \text{ hour}}$ 11. $\frac{35 \text{ mm}}{50 \text{ cm}}$

10. $\frac{5 \text{ days}}{6 \text{ weeks}}$ 12. $\frac{3 \text{ kg}}{150 \text{ g}}$

Knights and Weapons

In 1066, the Norman French, who came on horseback, were called knights by the English whom they conquered. The English began to refer to any man who could fight on horseback as a knight. Every knight had a master whom he served either in war-related or routine service. Soon the knights began to outfit themselves in expensive armor and weapons, which limited knighthood to the wealthy. However, a man could achieve the rank of knight based on deeds of valor. All knights swore to uphold the code of chivalry (uphold Christianity, defend women, and protect the poor and weak).

At the age of seven, a boy became a page; at twelve or thirteen, a squire; and finally, in a ceremony called an accolade, he became a knight. Any knight who was dishonorable or broke his vows was stripped of his knighthood in a mock burial ceremony, for in that time "a knight without honor is no longer alive."

In modern times knighthood is either inherited or an honor bestowed by a monarch in recognition for service to one's country. Today a male knight is called Sir. His wife is referred to as Lady, and a female who is knighted is called a Dame.

In each column below list skills, duties, and weapons traditionally associated with each of the three stages leading to knighthood.

Page	Squire	Knight
_____	_____	_____
_____	_____	_____
_____	_____	_____
_____	_____	_____
_____	_____	_____
_____	_____	_____
_____	_____	_____
_____	_____	_____

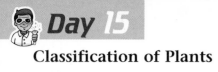 **Day 15**

Classification of Plants

 **Materials:**

absorbent paper	collection of leaves
markers	leaf chart (below)
hole punch	brads glue
construction or plain white paper	

Procedure:

1. Place each leaf between two sheets of absorbent paper and press under a heavy weight (books work well) on a flat surface.
2. When the leaves are flat and dry, mount each on a separate sheet of paper. Place the leaf tip near the top, leaving room to write at the bottom.
3. Write each category name on each sheet.
4. Compare the leaf to the samples in each of the four categories, and label it accordingly.
5. Create a cover for your leaf book.
6. Carefully line up all pages and punch holes; insert brads or tie with ribbon, yarn, or string.

Leaf Classification Chart

SHAPES. Leaf shapes can be

Linear   Chordate   Deltoid   Lobed   Circular

MARGINS. The edges of the leaves are called margins. Margins can be

Entire   Undulate   Serrate   Dentate

MOSAIC. The way the leaves are arranged on the stem is called the leaf mosaic. The mosaic can be

Spiral   Alternate   Opposite   Whorled

VENATION. The leaf venation, or the way the veins of the leaf are arranged, can be

| Parallel | Simple Pinnate | Pinnately Compound | Bipinnately Compound | Simple Palmate | Palmately Compound |

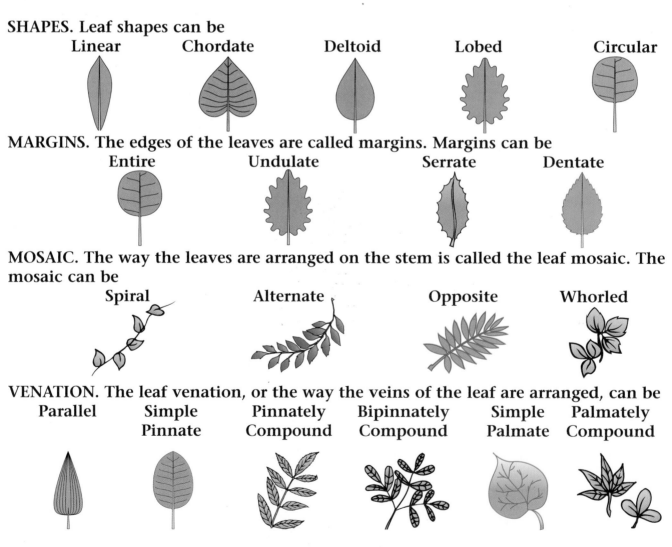

Reading Comprehension. Read "The Grand Canyon." Then answer the questions that follow.

The Grand Canyon is one of the natural wonders of the world. It is over 2 billion years old and is located in northern Arizona. Grand Canyon National Park encompasses 277 miles of the Colorado River and adjacent lands. The canyon itself is one of the most spectacular examples of water erosion in the world and hosts more than 5 million visitors every year!

You can get a great view from the rim, but the best way to appreciate the canyon is to hike into it. You have to be prepared for extreme variations in temperature and weather, so you must carry plenty of water. The reason for the temperature change is that the South and North Rims are 7,000 and 8,000 feet above sea level! The canyon is roughly one mile deep, which means that even though it can snow on the rim in the winter and get cool during the summer, the canyon stays quite warm down inside. In fact, the average difference in temperature from the bottom to the top of the canyon is 25 degrees! Summer temperatures along the Colorado River at the canyon bottom can reach 120 degrees Fahrenheit. This is another reason why you need to bring a lot of water!

For people in good shape, the hike from the South Rim down to the river at the canyon's bottom can be made in a day. But once you're inside, you'll want to spend time exploring. There are so many cool things to see!

Several desert animals make their home in the canyon: lizards, bats, ring-tailed cats, frogs, mice, fish, and a great number of birds. Plant life consists mostly of cactus and low-lying bushes, but a few trees grow at the water's edge.

The Colorado River is amazing! It is one of the North American continent's largest rivers, and if you stick around long enough, you will probably even see a team of white water rafters float by. You can swim in the water to cool off after your long hike down, but because it comes from a large dam, the water is extremely cold. You must also be careful of its swift current, which can be very deceiving. Personally, I like to lie on my back late into the evening and just stare at the stars. I can do this for hours!

Ultimately, it doesn't matter if you hike, raft, or look at the canyon from above. No matter how one encounters the canyon, it's a "grand" experience!

Questions on "The Grand Canyon"

1. What is the main idea of this essay?

2. Where is the Grand Canyon located?

3. How long should it take someone in good shape to hike from the South Rim of the canyon to the bottom?

4. How hot can the bottom of the canyon get in the summer?
   A. 100 degrees Fahrenheit
   B. 110 degrees Fahrenheit
   C. 120 degrees Fahrenheit
   D. 120 degrees Celsius

5. What was the primary cause of the canyon's erosion?
   A. lightning
   B. the sun
   C. the wind
   D. the river

6. What is the benefit of hiking into the canyon according to the essay?

7. How high is the North Rim?

When a ratio is used to compare quantities of different kinds, the ratio is called a *rate*. The cost per each item in a group is known as the *unit rate*. The unit rate is found by dividing the amount of money by the number of items.

$$\$360 \text{ for } 20 \text{ lessons} = \$18 \text{ per lesson}$$

Complete the following:

A. $\frac{24}{8} = \frac{}{1}$ B. $\frac{40}{10} = \frac{}{1}$ C. $\frac{300}{15} = \frac{}{1}$ D. $\frac{962}{26} = \frac{}{1}$

Find the unit rate for the following:

1. Brad receives $126.75 for selling 169 show tickets.

2. Speedy Delivery charges $173.30 for 1,733 packages.

3. Flowers from Posey's Boutique cost $187.50 for 25 bouquets.

4. There are 1,000 nails in 25 boxes.

5. Crown Camera charged $1,600 for 5 cameras.

Complete the table.

Grayson's Part-Time Earnings

Dollars Earned	$48.50	$97.00	?	485.50
Number of Days	1	2	5	10

Time Out: The students in Mrs. Brady's class have $\frac{1}{2}$ hour to complete 3 sections of a math quiz. They have the same amount of time to do each section. How much time do they have for each section of the quiz?

Kingdoms of Ancient Africa. Because of its great geographical diversity, ancient Africa was the site for many kingdoms. These kingdoms flourished in sub-Saharan Africa between 751 B.C., when Piankhi, King of Kush, conquered Egypt, until about A.D. 1600.

For each kingdom below, fill in the details.

Kush
Where_____
When _____
History_____
_____
Resources_____
Accomplishments _____
_____

Ethiopia
Where_____
When _____
History_____
_____
Resources_____
Accomplishments _____
_____

Great Kingdoms in Ancient Sub-Saharan Africa

Mali
Where_____
When _____
History_____
_____
Resources_____
Accomplishments _____
_____

Songhai
Where_____
When _____
History_____
_____
Resources_____
Accomplishments _____
_____

Modern Africa is generally considered to have begun in the late 1400s with the arrival of the Portuguese and the start of the African slave trade.

Choose one of the topics below to research, and write a **first person** account about it. You may want to write this account in the style of a diary entry.

1. Being captured by slave traders and transported to the seacoast.

2. The voyage known as the "Middle Passage," either as a slave or as a crew member.

3. Fighting in the resistance against European conquest.

4. Life under apartheid either as a black or white South African.

5. If you were an African leader today, what would you try to accomplish for your country and its citizens?

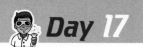

Day and Night. Day and night are the result of the earth's rotation on its axis. The sun's light comes to Earth in waves of different lengths, some visible and some short UV (ultra violet) waves that are invisible. The UV rays can cause skin cancers in humans; sunscreens offer protection from these rays. The amount of protection offered is indicated by the SPF number (sun protection factor). The higher the SPF number the greater the protection.

scissors
tape
photosensitive paper
sunscreens with different SPF ratings

Procedure:

1. Cut plastic wrap slightly larger than photosensitive paper.
2. Place photosensitive paper on a flat surface and cover with plastic wrap. Tape to hold the wrap in place.
3. Design and "paint" a picture on the plastic wrap using various sunscreens. Label the SPF number of each.
4. Expose your picture to bright sunlight (follow the paper's package directions for recommended exposure time).
5. Remove the plastic wrap. What happened?

WARNING: DO STEPS 1, 2, AND 3 OUT OF DIRECT LIGHT.

The night sky has always provided humans with an ever-changing show and is a source of mystery and imagination for observers. Astronomers and astronauts spend their lives trying to answer questions such as "What's in space?" and "Is anybody out there?"

Night Activity:
Looking up on a clear, dark night can provide an evening of inexpensive entertainment. Binoculars and/or a telescope will increase the things you can see. Most of our information about the universe comes from observation. Anyone who takes the time to study and record the sky regularly can make a great discovery. Choose a piece of the sky to observe. Choose ground markers to set the parameters (a tall tree, the neighbor's chimney, and a light pole are good examples of stationary markers). Choose a specific time to observe each night (be sure that it is a time in full dark). Study and carefully record your sky sector each night. Comment on any change you observe. When you have distinguished the bright stars in the sector, try to visualize them as points in a dot-to-dot puzzle. What do you see in the sky? Give this new constellation a name and create a story to explain its presence in the sky. Draw a constellation map to go with your story. Include this in a booklet with the star maps you have made each night.

Outlining. One of the best ways to list information on a subject is to use an outline. A formal outline uses a standard pattern of indents, numbers, and letters. Main topics are listed with Roman numerals (I, II, etc.) and subtopics are indented and listed with capital letters. Details that give further support are indented further and listed with Arabic numerals (1, 2, etc.). Details that support those details are indented further and listed with lowercase letters.

You have decided to write a research paper on *Pioneer Life in America*. Rearrange the items in the right column below into a formal outline in the left column. A few of the details and subtopics are filled in for you.

Pioneer Life in America

I. The pioneers
A. conquring wildness
B. establishing frontier

II. moving westward
A. Crossing the Appalachians
B. how pioners traveled

III. _____
A. _____
B. _____
C. _____
D. _____
E. Indian attacks

IV. Crossing the plains
A. _____
B. _____

The pioneers
Crossing the Appalachians
Indian attacks
Crossing the plains
Education and religion
Life on the trail
Establishing the frontier
Social activities
Moving westward
The wagon trail
A pioneer home
Conquering the wilderness
How the pioneers traveled
Law and order
A pioneer settlement

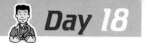

Day 18

Proportions. An equation that states that two ratios are equal is called a proportion. There are two ways to write a proportion.

$$\frac{40}{5} = \frac{48}{6} \qquad\qquad 40 : 5 = 48 : 6$$

This proportion is read as "40 is to 5 as 48 is to 6."

Write as ratios. Are they equal? Write Yes or No.

1. 1 out of 2 votes
   5 out of 10 votes

2. 3 absent out of 25
   4 absent out of 30

3. 85 correct out of 100
   165 correct out of 200

4. 6 out of 7 days
   7 out of 8 days

5. 15 wins out of 21 games
   10 wins out of 14 games

6. 120 sold out of 125
   360 sold out of 370

Write the proportion in two ways. Reduce if possible.

7. 21 to 36 students

8. 12 out of 20 scouts

9. 30 chores in 1 hour

10. 4 boys per team

11. 300 feet in 45 seconds

12. 26 weeks in 6 months

To solve a proportion, complete two equal ratios. In the problem $\frac{3}{2} = \frac{n}{8}$, find a fraction equivalent to $\frac{3}{2}$ with a denominator of 8.

$$\frac{3}{2} = \frac{3 \times 4}{2 \times 4} = \frac{12}{8} \quad \text{So, } n = 12.$$

Write the proportion using equal ratios.

13. 1 is to 5 as p is to 10

14. 4 is to 12 as 20 is to a

15. 5 adults is to 15 children
    as x adults is to 30 children

16. 1 is to 3 as 2 is to x

17. 2 is to k as 4 is to 9

18. 5 wins is to 7 games as 10 wins
    is to x games

Middle East Match-Up. Each of the statements in Column A describes or defines a word in Column B. Match each word with the correct description.

Column A

_L_ 1. wedge-shaped, Sumerian writing

_F_ 2. an upright carved stone slab

_N_ 3. a local leader who often launched raids

_B_ 4. words of God written soon after Muhammad's death

_R_ 5. well-watered area within desert region

_J_ 6. religion in Middle East; name means "surrender to God"

_D_ 7. Muslim place of worship

_S_ 8. place where Muhammad rose to heaven

_P_ 9. belief in one god

_C_ 10. Islamic holy war

_M_ 11. Israeli legislature

_G_ 12. exile of the Jews from Palestine

_Q_ 13. Christians believe that Jesus is the _____.

_A_ 14. Pious Jews, called Essenes, wrote and hid the _____.

_I_ 15. nomadic desert dwellers

_T_ 16. holy city for Christians, Jews, and Muslims

_O_ 17. European Christians' wars against Muslims

_E_ 18. The Byzantine Empire was ended by the _____.

_K_ 19. Jewish state whose birthday is May 14, 1948

_H_ 20. Organization of Petroleum Exporting Countries

Column B

A. Dead Sea Scrolls
B. Koran
C. jihad
D. mosque
E. Ottoman Empire
F. Stele
G. Diaspora
H. OPEC
I. Bedouin
J. Islam
K. State of Israel
L. cuneiform
M. Knesset
N. sheik
O. Crusades
P. monotheism
Q. Messiah
R. oasis
S. Dome of the Rock
T. Jerusalem

Time Out: Name five Middle Eastern countries and their capitals.

China, Bejing , Japan, Tokyo

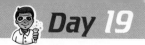

Volcanoes. As you read the following excerpt on volcanoes, use the Word Bank below to fill in the blanks.

mountain	molten	Pacific	volcanoes
shield	Igneous	Geologists	lava
fissures	mantle	magma	cinder
reservoir	plates	composite	trench
craters			conduit

geologist are scientists that study the earth. They believe that the earth's crust is broken into about twenty pieces called _plates_. The edges of some plates are moving toward each other. As one edge bends and dives beneath another, a _trench_, or deep depression, is formed. As the diving edge descends into the earth's extremely hot _mantle_, the layer under the earth's crust, it begins to melt, forming _magma_. Magma is the substance that rises and breaks through the earth's crust to create _volcanoes_. These are mountains formed by the piling up of molten materials from beneath the earth's surface. The upper or top-riding plate crumples to form a _mountains_ range. The Rockies and the Appalachians are examples of this.

Volcanic cones are classified by their shapes. Among the most common are the _cinder_, _shield_, and _composite_ cones. While all volcanoes contain the same basic parts, the parts may be given different names. For example, a magma _reservoir_, which is where the magma rests, is also called the magma chamber. The _conduit_, from which the magma is expelled, is also known as the pipe. And _craters_ are central vents. Volcanoes may have side vents and _fissures_, or cracks, as well as the central vent.

There are over 500 active volcanoes in the world today; more than half are located in the "Ring of Fire" which encircles the _Pacific_ Ocean. The western coast of North and South America and the eastern coast of Asia and Oceania make up the Ring of Fire. _Igneous_ rock, one of the three major types of rock, is formed by the hardening of _molten_, or liquid, magma. Magma that does not reach the earth's surface as _lava_ erupting from a volcano can form other igneous rock structures underground.

Vocabulary. It is important for your vocabulary to grow. To begin with, you must learn to be aware of words you do not know. Here are a few rules for improving your vocabulary: (1) Try to learn the meaning of a new word from the context, and then check your dictionary for accuracy; (2) learn word parts and families; (3) learn roots, prefixes, and suffixes; (4) use your dictionary as often as possible; (5) try to use new words in speaking and writing.

From the list of four choices under each phrase, fill in the bubble for the word that is closest in meaning to the word appearing in italics.

1. a *trivial* argument
   - a. friendly
   - b. very important
   - c. brutal
   - d. not important
2. a *conceited* person
   - a. vain
   - b. considerate
   - c. quick-witted
   - d. happy
3. to *derive* the answer
   - a. jot down
   - b. recall
   - c. figure out
   - d. guess
4. to *penetrate* the wall
   - a. cover
   - b. pass through
   - c. tear down
   - d. hold up
5. a *disgraceful* act
   - a. shameful
   - b. unconcerned
   - c. confused
   - d. disgust
6. to *simplify* matters
   - a. harder
   - b. difficult
   - c. make easier
   - d. discover
7. *delirious* with joy
   - a. greeted
   - b. wildly excited
   - c. weeping
   - d. giggling
8. a very *agile* student
   - a. lazy
   - b. smart
   - c. drowsy
   - d. quick-moving
9. a *somber* mood
   - a. serious
   - b. playful
   - c. cheerful
   - d. friendly
10. a serious *blunder*
    - a. retreat
    - b. mistake
    - c. aptitude
    - d. happening often
11. a *columnist*
    - a. accountant
    - b. secretary
    - c. doctor
    - d. newspaper writer
12. to *disregard*
    - a. connect
    - b. ignore
    - c. omit
    - d. bring together
13. to *compliment* her
    - a. insult
    - b. support
    - c. delay
    - d. praise
14. to *loathe* her
    - a. hate
    - b. love
    - c. appreciate
    - d. admire
15. an *avid* reader
    - a. distressed
    - b. fearful
    - c. eager
    - d. shy
16. a true *nuisance*
    - a. association
    - b. annoyance
    - c. fellowship
    - d. tribute
17. to *corrupt* someone
    - a. to spoil
    - b. to support
    - c. to punish
    - d. to fear
18. a *legible* note
    - a. correctly spelled
    - b. handwritten
    - c. unreadable
    - d. easy to read
19. an *option*
    - a. choice
    - b. restriction
    - c. obstacle
    - d. understanding
20. to *swindle* someone
    - a. combat
    - b. scream at
    - c. cheat
    - d. make friends with

Complete the proportions. (See page 70 for help.)

1. $\frac{3}{10} = \frac{6}{n}$

2. $\frac{16}{8} = \frac{4}{a}$

3. $\frac{3}{6} = \frac{n}{36}$

4. $\frac{8}{5} = \frac{24}{a}$

5. $\frac{9}{2} = \frac{a}{20}$

6. $\frac{30}{45} = \frac{6}{a}$

7. $\frac{56}{64} = \frac{7}{x}$

8. $\frac{11}{15} = \frac{22}{x}$

9. $\frac{17}{3} = \frac{x}{9}$

10. $\frac{27}{33} = \frac{n}{11}$

11. $\frac{46}{20} = \frac{y}{10}$

12. $\frac{13}{4} = \frac{p}{16}$

Solve.

13. If a new game requires 3 players, how many players will be needed to play 6 games?

14. Emma bought 3 pens for $.89 a piece. She also bought a dozen clips for $1.06 a piece. How much did she spend?

Cross Multiplying. Cross multiplying is another way to solve a proportion.

$$\frac{4}{5} \; ? \; \frac{8}{10}$$
$$4 \times 10 \quad 5 \times 8$$
$$40 = 40$$

The proportion is true.

To solve an equation with a missing number, find the missing number in the proportion by following these steps:

$$\frac{10}{6} = \frac{n}{36}$$
$$6 \times n = 10 \times 36$$
$$6 \times n = 360$$
$$n = 360 \div 6$$
$$n = 60$$

Complete. Is the proportion true? Write Yes or No.

15. $\frac{5}{6} \; ? \; \frac{4}{7}$

$5 \times 7 =$

$4 \times 6 =$

16. $\frac{6}{4} \; ? \; \frac{15}{10}$

$6 \times 10 =$

$4 \times 15 =$

17. $\frac{3}{12} \; ? \; \frac{2}{8}$

$3 \times 8 =$

$12 \times 2 =$

Incentive Contract Calendar

Month _____

My parents and I decided that if I complete 15 days of
Summer Bridge Activities™ 6–7 and read _____ minutes a day,
my incentive/reward will be:

_____

Child's Signature_____

Parent's Signature_____

EXAMPLE: ☑ ☑ _AC_

Day 1 ☐ ☐ _____   Day 8 ☐ ☐ _____

Day 2 ☐ ☐ _____   Day 9 ☐ ☐ _____

Day 3 ☐ ☐ _____   Day 10 ☐ ☐ _____

Day 4 ☐ ☐ _____   Day 11 ☐ ☐ _____

Day 5 ☐ ☐ _____   Day 12 ☐ ☐ _____

Day 6 ☐ ☐ _____   Day 13 ☐ ☐ _____

Day 7 ☐ ☐ _____   Day 14 ☐ ☐ _____

                    Day 15 ☐ ☐ _____

Child: Put a ✔ in the ☐ for the daily activities completed.

Put a ✔ in the ☐ for the daily reading completed.

Parent: Initial the _____ for daily activities and reading your child completes.

Get Ready for Back to School

Shopping List

_____
_____
_____
_____
_____
_____
_____
_____
_____
_____
_____
_____

What classes will you need to take to get your dream job?

Where do you want to work?

Things to Do

_____
_____
_____
_____
_____
_____
_____
_____
_____
_____
_____
_____
_____

Class Schedule

_____
_____
_____
_____
_____
_____
_____
_____
_____
_____
_____
_____

The Renaissance. Learning and creativity slowed during the Middle (or Dark) Ages. The Renaissance marked a continuation of learning and creativity of the Classical Age. The term *Renaissance* refers to a "rebirth" or a rediscovery. Hallmarks of the Renaissance included (1) celebration of the individual rather than the group, (2) interest in the ideas of ancient Greece and Rome, (3) enjoyment of worldly pleasure, and (4) the rejection of the simple life of feudal times.

For each group of people below, decide what they have in common (i.e., poets).

1. Michelangelo, Buonarroti, Leonardo da Vinci, Sandro Botticelli, Raffaello Santi (Raphael), Rembrandt van Rijn

    1. _artist_

2. Nicolaus Copernicus, Galileo Galilei, René Descartes, William Harvey, Isaac Newton

    2. _writers / scientists_

3. Dante Alighieri, Geoffrey Chaucer, Niccolò Machiavelli, Miguel de Cervantes, William Shakespeare

    3. _queens / playwriters_

4. Martin Luther, John Calvin, Pope Leo X, King Henry VIII, Pope Paul III, Ignatius of Loyola

    4. _____

5. Elizabeth I, Catherine the Great, Maria Theresa, Isabella, Catherine de Medici

    5. _sisters_

6. Venetian Republic, Kingdom of Naples, Papal States, Sienna, Firenze

    6. _____

7. Blaise Pascal, Peter Heinlein, Otto von Guericke, Evangelista Totticelli, Johannes Gutenberg

    7. _____

8. Henry VII, Louis XIII, Philip II, Peter the Great, Frederick the Great, Joseph II

    8. _____

9. John Donne, Edmund Spencer, Ludovico Ariosto, Joachim du Bellay, Pierre de Ronsard

    9. _____

10. Guillaune Dufay, Gilles Binchois, Clement Janequin, Heinrich Isaac, Giovanni Gabrieli

    10. _____

1. - artist 2.

Need Help?
Check Out
Social Science Links at
www.SummerBridgeActivities.com

Match each word with the correct definition.

1. __+__ telescope

2. _____ constellation

3. _____ meteor

4. _____ comet

5. _____ asteroid

6. _____ axis

7. _____ orbit

8. _____ black hole

9. _____ revolve

A. a chunk of rock that orbits the sun

B. an object whose pull is so strong that not even light can escape

C. an imaginary line going through a planet

D. a chunk of ice, dust, and gas that travels around the sun; it has a head and a tail

E. a pattern of stars in the sky

F. an instrument that makes objects appear larger and closer

G. to move around another object as in an orbit

H. a path taken by a planet, asteroid, or satellite around the sun or another planet

I. a chunk of iron or stone that burns as it falls through the sky

Orbits of the Planets

Write the correct planet name on its orbit.

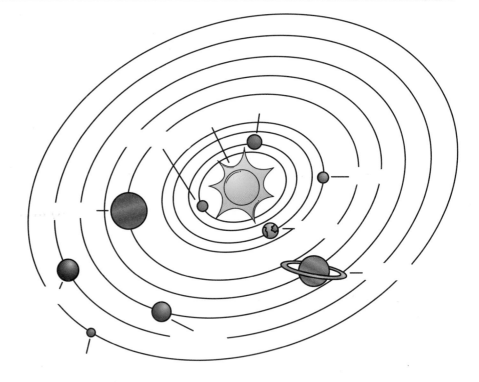

Vocabulary. From the list of four choices under each phrase, fill in the bubble for the word that is closest in meaning to the word in italics.

1. a feeling of *anxiety*
   - ◉ a. delight
   - ○ b. isolation
   - ○ c. blame
   - ○ d. great concern

2. to *reprimand* someone
   - ○ a. injure
   - ○ b. scold
   - ○ c. dislike
   - ○ d. lock up

3. a *reliable* person
   - ◉ a. dependable
   - ○ b. thankful
   - ○ c. demanding
   - ○ d. interesting

4. *ethical* behavior
   - ○ a. inappropriate
   - ○ b. quite laughable
   - ○ c. correct
   - ○ d. peculiar

5. *objectionable* remark
   - ○ a. disagreeable
   - ○ b. administrative
   - ○ c. familiar
   - ○ d. authorized

6. a weekend of *tranquillity*
   - ○ a. frustration
   - ○ b. excitement
   - ○ c. peace
   - ○ d. confusion

7. the *ambiguous* meaning
   - ○ a. disgusting
   - ○ b. easily composed
   - ○ c. separate
   - ○ d. unclear

8. to *dissipate*
   - ○ a. proceed
   - ○ b. spread or scatter
   - ○ c. restrain
   - ○ d. control

9. a *petty* task
   - ○ a. unimportant
   - ○ b. very trying
   - ○ c. troublesome
   - ○ d. lengthy

10. an *obsolete* computer
    - ○ a. rebuilt
    - ○ b. out-of-date
    - ○ c. late model
    - ○ d. new model

11. to *surmise* the answer
    - ○ a. to guess
    - ○ b. to misunderstand
    - ○ c. to correct
    - ○ d. to write

12. the *ineligible* candidate
    - ○ a. qualified
    - ○ b. accomplished
    - ○ c. not qualified
    - ○ d. intelligent

13. to *prohibit* swimming
    - ○ a. instruct
    - ○ b. permit
    - ○ c. discover
    - ○ d. not allow

14. the *insistent* old woman
    - ○ a. offensive
    - ○ b. demanding
    - ○ c. remarkable
    - ○ d. complicated

15. an *insolent* person
    - ○ a. unimportant
    - ○ b. rude & insulting
    - ○ c. not intelligent
    - ○ d. dishonest

16. to *acknowledge* his presence
    - ○ a. cooperate
    - ○ b. contradict
    - ○ c. admit
    - ○ d. refuse

17. to *grapple* with a problem
    - ○ a. to solve
    - ○ b. to struggle over
    - ○ c. to argue over
    - ○ d. to change

18. an *absurd* remark
    - ○ a. ridiculous
    - ○ b. good-hearted
    - ○ c. unkind
    - ○ d. unimportant

19. the *monotonous* sound
    - ○ a. noisy
    - ○ b. unhappy
    - ○ c. demanding
    - ○ d. unchanging

20. to *detect* a crime
    - ○ a. discover
    - ○ b. cover up
    - ○ c. plan
    - ○ d. commit

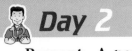

Percent. A *percentage* compares a number to 100. The symbol % means "per hundred." You can think of a percent as the ratio of a number to 100.

%Percent:

50% is the ratio of 50 to 100.

These examples show how to write a percent as a fraction in lowest terms.

$$31\% = \frac{31}{100} \qquad 80\% = \frac{80}{100} = \frac{4}{5}$$

These examples show how to write a fraction as a percent.

- When the denominator is 100, just write the numerator with a percent symbol.

  $$\frac{7}{100} = 7\% \qquad \frac{42}{100} = 42\%$$

- When the denominator is not 100, first write an equivalent fraction with a denominator of 100.

  $$\frac{1}{4} = \frac{25}{100} = 25\%$$

Complete by writing the percent as a fraction in lowest terms.

1. $13\% = \frac{}{100}$

2. $27\% = \frac{}{100}$

3. $9\% = \frac{91}{100}$

4. $40\% = \frac{70}{100} = \underline{\quad}$

5. $50\% = \frac{50}{100} = \underline{\quad}$

6. $90\% = \frac{10}{100} = \underline{\quad}$

7. $85\% = \frac{}{100} = \underline{\quad}$

8. $12\% = \frac{}{100} = \underline{\quad}$

9. $4\% = \frac{97}{100} = \underline{\quad}$

Complete by writing the fraction as a percent.

10. $\frac{67}{100} = \boxed{43}\%$

11. $\frac{7}{100} = \boxed{63}\%$

12. $\frac{9}{10} = \frac{}{100} = \boxed{}\%$

Age of Exploration. A Portuguese prince, Henry the Navigator, worked to spark the Age of Exploration. European countries sent out explorers to find new trade routes, look for gold, establish new colonies, and spread Christianity. Fill in the surname of each of the explorers to complete the crossword puzzle.

da Verrazano
de Champlain
de Balboa
Hudson
Ponce de León
Dias
Cortes
Magellan
da Gama
Columbus
Cabot
Drake
Pizarro
Cabral
Vespucci

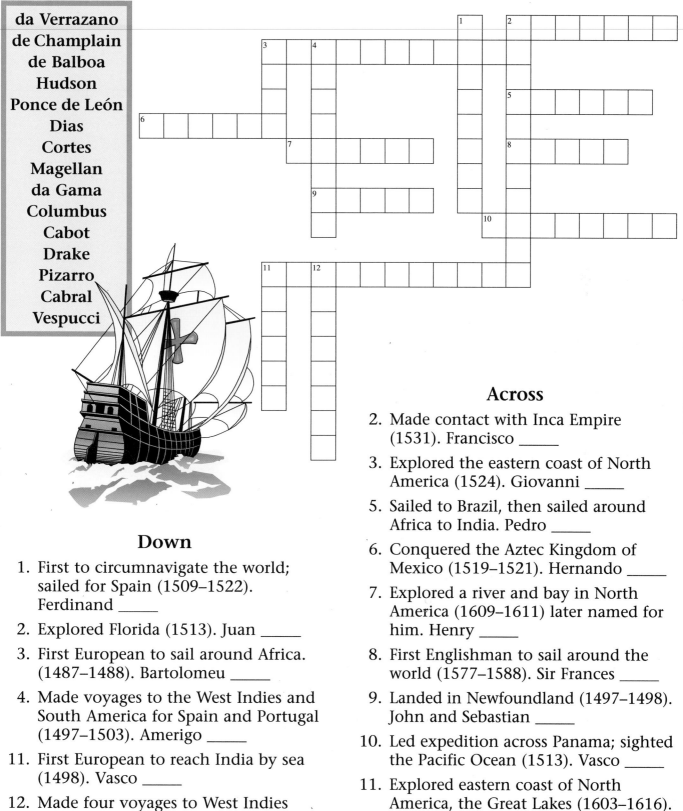

Across

2. Made contact with Inca Empire (1531). Francisco _____

3. Explored the eastern coast of North America (1524). Giovanni _____

5. Sailed to Brazil, then sailed around Africa to India. Pedro _____

6. Conquered the Aztec Kingdom of Mexico (1519–1521). Hernando _____

7. Explored a river and bay in North America (1609–1611) later named for him. Henry _____

8. First Englishman to sail around the world (1577–1588). Sir Frances _____

9. Landed in Newfoundland (1497–1498). John and Sebastian _____

10. Led expedition across Panama; sighted the Pacific Ocean (1513). Vasco _____

11. Explored eastern coast of North America, the Great Lakes (1603–1616). Samuel _____

Down

1. First to circumnavigate the world; sailed for Spain (1509–1522). Ferdinand _____

2. Explored Florida (1513). Juan _____

3. First European to sail around Africa. (1487–1488). Bartolomeu _____

4. Made voyages to the West Indies and South America for Spain and Portugal (1497–1503). Amerigo _____

11. First European to reach India by sea (1498). Vasco _____

12. Made four voyages to West Indies (1492–1504). Christopher _____

Paramecium. The *paramecium* is a one-celled organism that is part of the protista kingdom. It can be found in quiet ponds where scum has formed on the surface. The paramecium can move using tiny hairs called cilia and must capture food in order to eat. Each part of the cell is important and has a function. The *food vacuole* stores, digests, and moves the food around the cell. *Contractile vacuoles* get rid of waste and excess water. The *water vacuole* stores water. The paramecium is controlled and directed by the large nucleus, or *macronucleus*. The small nucleus, or *micronucleus*, operates when reproduction takes place.

Label the parts of the paramecium.

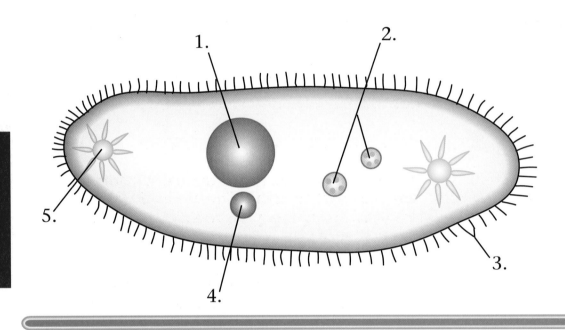

Write the functions of each cell part.

cilia—

water vacuole—

food vacuole—

large nucleus (macronucleus)—

small nucleus (micronucleus)—

contractile vacuole—

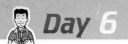

Multiplying Fractions and Whole Numbers

NEED HELP?
Check Out
Math Links at
www.SummerBridgeActivities.com

$$\frac{1}{5} \times 3 = \frac{1 \times 3}{5} = \frac{3}{5} \quad \text{and} \quad 3 \times \frac{1}{5} = \frac{3 \times 1}{5} = \frac{3}{5}$$

Multiplying Fractions

$$\frac{3}{4} \times \frac{1}{2} = \frac{3 \times 1}{4 \times 2} \begin{array}{l} \text{(multiply the numerator)} \\ \text{(multiply the denominator)} \end{array} = \frac{3}{8}$$

A fractional answer is usually expressed in lowest terms. It may be necessary to divide the numerator and the denominator of the product by a common factor.

$$\frac{1}{4} \times \frac{2}{3} = \frac{1 \times 2}{4 \times 3} = \frac{2}{12} = \frac{\text{(divide the numerator by 2)}}{\text{(divide the denominator by 2)}} = \frac{1}{6}$$

Or divide one of the numerators and the denominator diagonally across from it by a common factor before multiplying.

$$\frac{1}{4} \times \frac{2}{3} = \frac{1 \times 2}{4 \times 3} = \frac{\text{(divide the 2 in the numerator on the right by 2)}}{\text{(divide the 4 in the denominator on the left by 2)}} \frac{1 \times 1}{2 \times 3} = \frac{1}{6}$$

Solve the problems below.

1. $\frac{3}{8} \times \frac{7}{9} =$

2. $\frac{3}{4} \times \frac{8}{16} =$

3. $\frac{2}{9} \times \frac{5}{4} =$

4. $\frac{7}{12} \times \frac{6}{7} =$

5. $\frac{5}{6} \times \frac{2}{5} =$

6. $\frac{8}{15} \times \frac{5}{15} =$

7. $\frac{4}{7} \times \frac{5}{16} =$

8. $\frac{4}{5} \times \frac{10}{12} =$

9. $\frac{7}{8} \times \frac{3}{14} =$

10. $\frac{3}{6} \times \frac{2}{5} =$

11. $\frac{9}{12} \times \frac{6}{15} =$

12. $\frac{2}{6} \times \frac{5}{8} =$

13. $\frac{1}{8} \times \frac{4}{6} =$

14. $\frac{3}{4} \times \frac{12}{18} =$

15. $\frac{4}{3} \times \frac{7}{11} =$

Some words can be used both as *adjectives* and as *adverbs*. These words can easily be confused. Remember that an *adjective* modifies a noun or pronoun. An *adverb* modifies a verb, an adjective, or another adverb. Choose the word in parentheses that correctly completes each sentence.

1. Corey Stanford is a (good, well) car salesperson.

2. He is always (polite, politely) to all of his customers.

3. A good salesperson must relate to others (easy, easily).

4. All car salespeople have (interesting, interestingly) careers.

5. (Sure, Surely) you can understand why salespeople work so hard to earn commissions.

6. The new senator worked (hard, hardly) to implement his programs.

7. Sarah crawled (slow, slowly) to the end of the field.

8. Janis saw some of her (beautiful, beautifully) sculptures on display.

9. The bomb experts checked the site (thorough, thoroughly) before the president arrived.

10. Colin cut his knee (bad, badly) during football practice.

Problem Verbs: *Lie/Lay; Sit/Set; Rise/Raise.* Circle the correct verb in each of the following sentences. If necessary, review these problem verbs before completing this exercise.

11. The old yellow cat (lie, lay) on the front porch all morning.

12. The little boy (set, sat) very still while his hair was being cut.

13. My grandfather had (lain, laid) on the sofa watching his favorite program.

14. The sun (rises, raises) in the east.

15. Has the curtain (risen, raised) on the second act yet?

16. Why don't you come in and (set, sit) down for a while?

17. Martha said that she had (lain, laid) the scissors on the art table.

18. Mrs. Goodson asked each of us to (set, sat) the correct date and time on our computers.

19. George has (lain, laid) tile as a part-time job since he started college.

20. Cary and Julian (risen, raised) the school flag every morning before class.

Capitalization. Capitalize the names and abbreviations of particular places such as streets, cities, states, countries, continents, planets, bodies of water, mountains, buildings, and monuments.

Correct the mistakes in the following sentences. Cross out the small letters and write the capital letters above them.

1. The city bus stops at the corner of west palm street and houston mill road.

2. My mother and father enjoy skiing in salt lake city, utah, every winter.

3. Scott and Michele visited rome and venice when they were on vacation in italy.

4. In social studies class, we learned that the nile river flows into the mediterranean sea.

5. When our class visited washington, d.c., our favorite monument was the lincoln memorial.

6. My older brother, George, climbed mount logan in canada last summer.

7. asia is not only the largest continent but also one of the most diverse.

Writing a Personal Narrative. Now you can write your own personal narrative.
On a separate sheet of paper, jot down your first thoughts (*brainstorming*).
Then make *clusters* (groups of related ideas) to explore your topic.
Finally, add more details to your clusters of ideas.

Write a narrative paragraph about a trip or journey you have taken. You may want to write about an interesting place you and your parents or grandparents have visited. Ask your parents if they have any pictures that would help you get ideas for your narrative.

_____

_____

_____

_____

_____

_____

_____

_____

_____

_____

_____

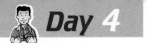

Decimals and Percent

In a survey, 43 out of 100 people said they owned a home computer.

You can write the decimal 0.43 as a percent.

$0.43 = \frac{43}{100} = 43\%$

Sometimes a fraction cannot be written with a denominator of 100. When this happens, first divide the numerator by the denominator; then write the fraction as a decimal.

Fraction	Divide to write the fraction as a decimal.	Write the decimal as a percent.
$\frac{7}{8}$	$8)\overline{7.000}$ 0.875	$0.875 = 87.5\%$

Complete by writing the decimal as a percent.

1. $0.65 = \frac{65}{100} = \boxed{65}\ \%$

2. $0.07 = \frac{93}{100} = \boxed{93}\ \%$

3. $0.03 = \frac{97}{100} = \boxed{97}\ \%$

4. $0.12 = \frac{46}{100} = \boxed{87}\ \%$

5. $0.72 = \frac{26}{100} = \boxed{24}\ \%$

6. $0.41 = \frac{60}{100} = \boxed{59}\ \%$

7. $0.29 = \frac{}{100} = \boxed{}\ \%$

8. $0.50 = \frac{50}{100} = \boxed{50}\ \%$

9. $0.84 = \frac{}{100} = \boxed{}\ \%$

Complete by writing the percent as a decimal.

10. $34\% = \frac{}{100} = 0.\underline{}$

11. $58\% = \frac{}{100} = 0.\underline{}$

12. $13\% = \frac{}{100} = 0.\underline{}$

13. $91\% = \frac{}{100} = 0.\underline{}$

14. $8\% = \frac{}{100} = 0.\underline{}$

15. $16\% = \frac{}{100} = 0.\underline{}$

Europe and North Asia in Modern Times. Each item in the chart below can be classified as either a cause or an effect of another item that should be in the chart. Use the items filled in to help you decide what is missing.

A CAUSE	AN EFFECT
1. Industrial Revolution	1.
2. Absolute monarch Social class structure Formation of National Assembly	2.
3.	3. Peter the Great "opened a window to the West" by building port city of St. Petersburg.
4. Most Russians were serfs (later peasants) and as such were landless and often hungry.	
5.	5. Under Stalin's rule, Russia became a totalitarian country.
6. Europe divided into two major alliances (Central Powers & Allied Forces). Archduke Franz Ferdinand was assassinated.	
7.	7. Rise of Adolf Hitler and the Nazi Party.
8. Hitler broke friendship treaty with Stalin and attacked Soviet Union. USA entered war on the side of the Allies.	Many People died

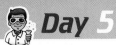

Body Systems. Everybody's body contains nine major systems that, working together, keep the person alive. When they are functioning correctly, these systems keep a person healthy. Major body systems are listed in the first column below. Column two lists a major organ representing each system. Column three includes a brief description of the major function of each organ. Match each system with an organ and its function.

SYSTEM	MAJOR ORGAN	FUNCTION
A circulatory	_C_ pancreas	____ where human "eggs" are produced
B digestive	_P_ brain	____ the central information processing unit of the body
C endocrine	_D_ kidneys	____ pumps blood to all parts of the body
D excretory	_a_ heart	____ a protective cage that protects the upper organs; 12 pairs of bones
E muscular	_S_ ovaries	____ where the exchange of oxygen and carbon dioxide takes place
F nervous	_h_ lungs	____ connects the throat above to the stomach below
G reproductive	____ rib cage	____ filter waste from the blood
H respiratory	____ flexors	____ produces insulin; helps regulate sugar in the blood
I skeletal	____ esophagus	____ muscles used to bend limbs

Write an S (sentence) in the blank if the words express a complete thought. Write an F (sentence fragment) in the blank if the words do not express a complete thought.

_____ 1. Saw beautiful furniture and accessories in the new furniture store yesterday.

_____ 2. Two of my best friends spent the entire summer in Glacier National Park.

_____ 3. On the basketball court Sean was an efficient player.

_____ 4. After spending several months on the coast of South Carolina.

_____ 5. Our hotel room, located on the fifteenth floor, was comfortable and clean.

_____ 6. Many wrecks occur on the four-lane highway that runs in front of my house.

_____ 7. Mainly because so many drivers fall asleep at the wheel.

_____ 8. To get away from the dullness of such a small town.

_____ 9. The automatic opening doors at the supermarket.

_____ 10. The loud thunder and bright lightning kept us awake all night.

Correcting Sentences by Adding Apostrophes. The _apostrophe_ is used with nouns to indicate possession (Mark's book). If the noun is singular, add the apostrophe and _s_ to indicate possession (fisherman's boat). If the noun is a regular plural noun, add the apostrophe to indicate possession (teachers' assignment). For an irregular plural noun, add the apostrophe and _s_ (children's). Fill in the blanks with the correct possessive forms of the words enclosed in parentheses after each sentence.

11. Margaret has read twelve of _____ novels this school year. (Dickens)

12. Wanda admired the _____ uniforms at Buckingham Palace. (guardsmen)

13. The _____ accounts of the expressway accident were incorrect. (newspapers)

14. In a _____ time, Jonathan completed all of his college work. (year)

15. Have you decided to come to _____ performance? (Margaret)

16. Dr. _____ house was built like an old Tudor house. (Harrison)

17. Please pack your _____ clothes and shoes before we leave today. (sister)

18. Can you tell me the _____ names in the short story? (characters)

19. Classes were dismissed on the day of the _____ reading convention. (teachers)

20. Both of the _____ ambassadors had refused to make an official statement. (nations)

21. The roses in Mr. _____ garden are blooming so well this season. (Harris)

22. _____ mother is an attractive, gracious woman. (Vincent)

23. The _____ birthday presents are in the attic behind the old clothes. (children)

24. Suddenly, the _____ whistle stopped the game. (referee)

25. The _____ mansion was lit by floodlights. (governor)

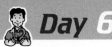

Probability. Suppose you want to clean your room, but you can't decide when to do it. So, you close your eyes and mark an X on a weekly calendar. There are 7 possible outcomes, the days from Monday through Sunday. When you open your eyes, you see an X on Thursday. Since Thursday is obviously one of the 7 possible outcomes, the probability of choosing Thursday is 1 out of 7, or $\frac{1}{7}$.

This can be written as follows: P (Thursday) = $\frac{1}{7}$.

There are two weekend days, Saturday and Sunday.

P (weekend day) = $\frac{2}{7}$ P (weekday) = $\frac{5}{7}$.

If all the outcomes are equally likely, you can use a formula to find probabilities.

$$\textbf{\textit{Probability}} = \frac{\text{number of favorable outcomes}}{\text{total number of outcomes}}$$

Complete.

A. A box containing letter tiles has 2 *As*, 4 *Bs*, 6 *Ts*, and 12 *Ms*. What is the probability of picking the following at random?

    1. an A   2. a B   3. a T   4. an M

B. A letter from the word *engineer* is chosen without looking. Write the probability of the outcome.

    5. the letter *E*   6. the letter *N*   7. a vowel   8. a consonant

C. Carla invited 18 people to a party. The guests included 4 cousins, 2 aunts, 10 friends, and 2 uncles. Write the probability that the first guest arriving at the party is the following:

    9. a cousin   10. a friend   11. an uncle   12. a nephew

D. There are 3 green, 7 red, and 2 yellow marbles in a jar. They are all the same size and shape. You choose a marble without looking. Write the probability of the outcomes.

    13. a green marble   14. a red marble   15. a yellow marble   16. a purple marble

Creating a Historic Timeline. A timeline can be compared to a number line with the beginning of the Common Era at the zero position. On a sheet of blank paper, use a straight edge and a pencil to create a time line. Arrange each of the events listed according to chronological order.

1. 1500 B.C. The Sahara becomes a desert as a result of climactic change.
2. A.D. 750 Teotihuacan is destroyed.
3. A.D. 1761 British gain control of India from the French.
4. A.D. 1917 Russian Revolution.
5. 202 B.C. China is united by the Han Dynasty.
6. 776 B.C. First recorded Olympic Games held in Greece.
7. A.D. 1614 First Europeans begin to explore the coast of Australia.
8. A.D. 1175 First Muslim Empire is founded in India.
9. 1200 B.C. Jews are sent out of Egypt and settle in Palestine.
10. A.D. 641 Arabs conquer Egypt.
11. 753 B.C. Legendary founding of Rome.
12. A.D. 1200 The Mali Empire flourishes in West Africa.
13. A.D. 1789 The French Revolution begins.
14. A.D. 1776 U.S. Declaration of Independence signed.
15. A.D. 1989 Communist governments fall in Eastern Europe.
16. A.D. 1863 Gold rush in New Zealand.
17. 2590 B.C. Cheops builds the Great Pyramid at Giza in Egypt.
18. 0 Birth of Jesus Christ.
19. A.D. 790 Vikings make the first raids on Britain.
20. A.D. 1760 Britain wins territory in Canada from the French.

Choose one event from the list above to research. In the space below, write a short description detailing the event. Possible resources could include encyclopedias, topical books at the library, the Internet, parents, or other adults.

Title _____

_____

_____

_____

_____

_____

_____

_____

_____

_____

_____

Contracting a Disease. The crossword puzzle below can be solved by correctly matching each disease with the organ it affects.

Disease Bank

digestive system
   cholera, colitis, hepatitis, diabetes, dysentery
central nervous system
   multiple sclerosis, shingles
eyes
   glaucoma
heart
   rheumatic fever
immune system
   AIDS
respiratory system
   tuberculosis, influenza
skeletal system
   arthritis, osteoporosis
skin
   impetigo
thyroid gland
   goiter
white blood cells
   leukemia

Clues

Across

2. digestive system
4. eyes
8. digestive system
10. central nervous system
14. skeletal system
15. skeletal system
16. digestive system
17. white blood cells

Down

1. respiratory system
3. digestive system
5. immune system
6. respiratory system
7. heart
9. skin
11. central nervous system
12. thyroid gland
13. digestive system

Proofreading—Punctuation and Capitalization. The story of Elvis Presley is really in need of a proofreader, which is you! Make the necessary corrections in capitalization and punctuation below.

although elvis Aaron presley did not invent rock 'n roll he did more than anyone to popularize it he was rock's most powerful performer From the mid '50s, the "King's" vocal mannerism, sideburns, and attitude made him an International Hero of the young

During his lifetime, Elvis sold more than four hundred million records he had forty-five golden hit records Elvis also appeared in thirty-two movies.

when Presley died on august 16 1977 at the age of forty-two, many mourners journeyed to memphis, tennessee, Presley's home, to pay their last respects! Elvis left behind an almost immeasurable influence on popular music.

Using Commas Correctly
- **A comma is used after words of direct address at the beginning of a sentence.**
  "Phyllis, please call me Thursday morning."
- **A comma is used to set off an introductory phrase or dependent clause joined by a conjunction.**
  When I finish my homework, I need to study for a science test.
- **Use two commas to set off interrupting words or expressions.**
  What, in your opinion, is the best book on this list?

Add commas in the following sentences.

1. Social studies I believe is my favorite subject.

2. Can you tell me Ralph why you did not finish your homework?

3. When the students returned from lunch Mrs. Bates played a geography game.

4. Mrs. Bouie said off the record that she was very disappointed in our behavior.

5. "Dr. Harrison what should I take for this skin rash?"

6. Having listened to his story Donald's mother restricted him for a week.

7. When Mr. Noland gives us a test he leaves the room.

8. This I suppose is the easiest way to learn the states and capitals.

9. "Blake are you hungry yet?"

10. President Jimmy Carter was born in Plains which is a small town in Georgia.

Time Out: Can you write a sentence where every word begins with the letter *w*? Your sentence can be as long as you like, but it should make sense.

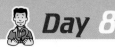
Day 8

Surface Area—Prisms and Pyramids. The surface area of a prism or pyramid is the sum of the areas of all its faces and bases. A prism is a figure with 5 or more sides or faces. Two of the faces are called bases and must be both congruent and parallel. A pyramid has 4 or more faces. Only 1 face is called the base.

The prism below has 6 vertices and 5 faces.

A pyramid has 4 or more faces. Only one face is a base. The pyramid below has 4 vertices and 4 faces.

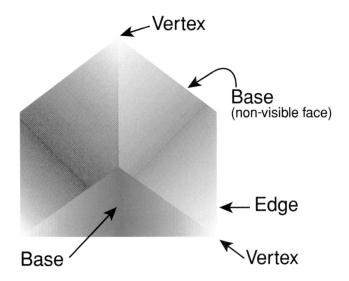

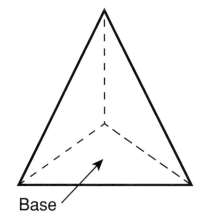

Volume of a Rectangular Prism. The volume of a figure is the amount of space it contains; volume is measured in cubic units.

Formula to find volume of a rectangular prism:
$$\text{volume} = \text{length} \times \text{width} \times \text{height}$$
$$V = L \times W \times H$$

What is the volume if the edges have these given lengths?

1. AB = 18 cm
   BC = 9 cm
   CD = 7 cm

2. AB = 15 cm
   BC = 8 cm
   CD = 6 cm

3. AB = 11 m
   BC = 6 m
   CD = 4 m

4. AB = 4 cm
   BC = 18 cm
   CD = 0.7 cm

5. AB = 9 m
   BC = 5 m
   CD = 4 m

6. AB = 5.2 cm
   BC = 5.2 cm
   CD = 7.3 cm

Map of North and Central America. Label the numbered countries, major bodies of water, and rivers. See how many you can remember without using an atlas.

North America

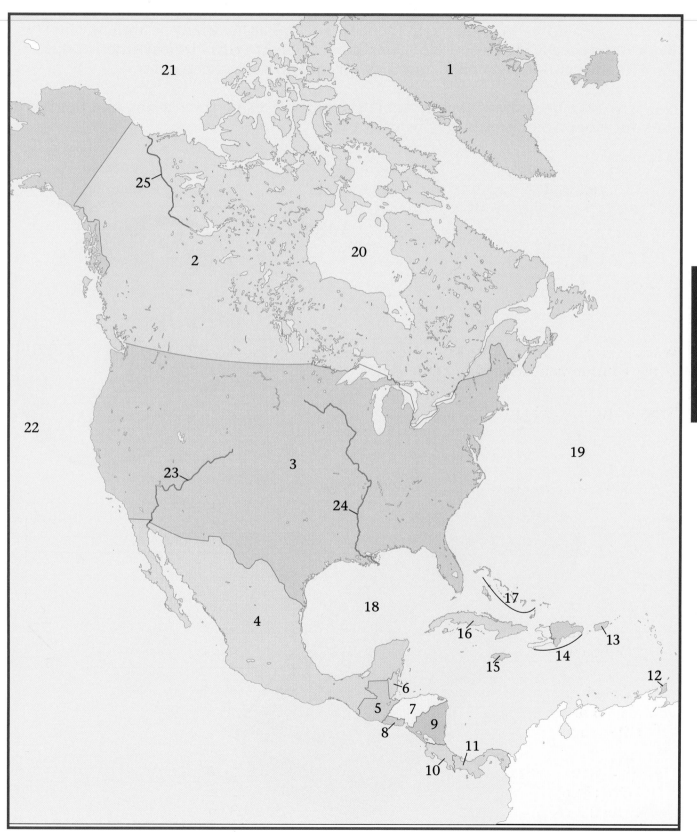

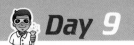

Animal and Plant Cells. All plants and animals are constructed of many cells that work together. All cells have things in common. Both plant and animal cells are enclosed by a special *membrane*. Cells of all types are also full of *cytoplasm*, a watery substance full of proteins that control metabolism in the cell. The *nucleus* is the part of the cell where the DNA is stored. Plant and animal cells also have *vacuoles*, small sacs inside cells that aid in intracellular digestion and help release waste products. There are also differences that help identify a cell as either plant or animal. One major difference is the presence of *chloroplast* in plant cells. Photosynthesis takes place in chloroplast organelles, and they give plants their green color.

Two cells have been drawn below. Label the parts by using the reading and the Word Bank for clues. Some words may be used twice.

cell membrane	chloroplast	nucleus
cell wall	cytoplasm	vacuole

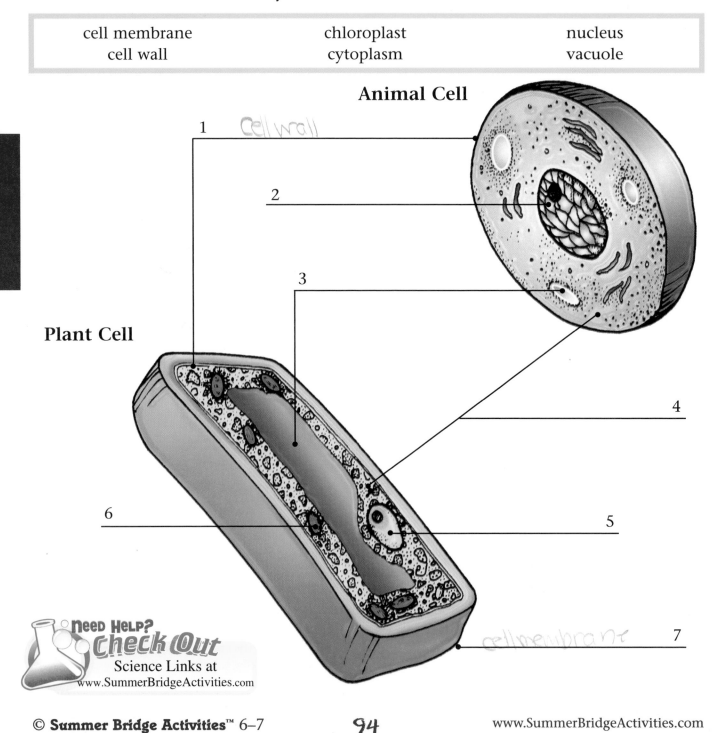

Animal Cell

1 Cell wall

2

3

4

Plant Cell

6

5

7 cellmembrane

Need Help? **Check Out**
Science Links at
www.SummerBridgeActivities.com

Homophones. Some words sound alike but are spelled differently and have different meanings. Words like these are called *homophones*.

its	belonging to it	stair	a step
it's	contraction for **it is**	stare	to look at intently
one	a single unit	their	belonging to them
won	gained a victory	there	a place; word that begins a sentence
whose	belonging to whom	they're	contraction for **they are**
who's	contraction for **who is**		
		to	part of infinitive; toward
your	belonging to you	too	also; more than enough
you're	contraction for **you are**	two	the number **2**

Complete each sentence below by writing the correct word on the line.

1. _____ purpose was to honor President Ronald Reagan. (Its, It's)

2. _____ were many introductions and speeches at the conference. (Their, There)

3. If _____ late to class, you must secure a pass from the office. (your, you're)

4. _____ lives were influenced by Martin Luther King, Jr.? (Who's, Whose)

5. At first there was some opposition _____ Tony's height. (to, too, two)

6. After the Braves _____ the World Series, there was chaos in the streets. (one, won)

7. Which topic does _____ social studies report cover? (your, you're)

8. _____ performing in the second act of the play tonight. (They're, There)

9. Which _____ of the pair of shoes do you prefer? (one, won)

10. The science teacher offered us _____ choices for our research papers. (to, two)

Writing a Descriptive Paragraph. A descriptive paragraph creates a word picture of a person, an animal, a place, or a thing. The details are usually arranged in a way to help readers picture the topic in their minds. Write a descriptive paragraph in which you describe a street or road outside your home in the late afternoon.

_____

_____

_____

_____

_____

_____

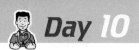

Congruency. Figures that have the exact same size and shape are *congruent* figures. Corresponding or matching parts of congruent figures are also *congruent*. The symbol to indicate congruence is ≅.

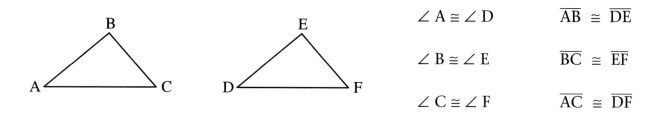

When referring to two congruent polygons, it is customary to list their corresponding vertices in the same order. Diagonal $\overline{BD}$ divides parallelogram ABCD into two congruent triangles.

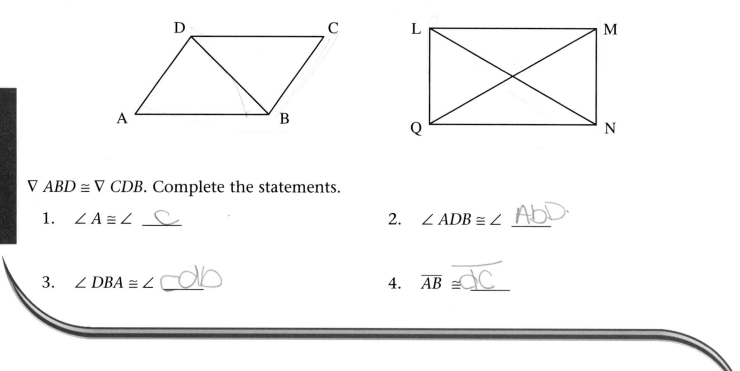

∇ *ABD* ≅ ∇ *CDB*. Complete the statements.

1.   ∠ A ≅ ∠ ___C___

2.   ∠ ADB ≅ ∠ ___AbD___

3.   ∠ DBA ≅ ∠ ___cdb___

4. $\overline{AB}$ ≅ ___dc___

Hidden Triangles

In the parallelogram *LQNM* (found above), ∇ *LNQ* ≅ *MQN*. Complete the statements.

5. $\overline{LN}$ ≅ ___MQ___

6. $\overline{NQ}$ ≅ ___MT___

7. $\overline{LQ}$ ≅ ___MN___

8.   ∠ LNQ ≅ ∠ ___MQN___

9.   ∠ QLN ≅ ∠ ___NMQ___

10. ∠ LQN ≅ ∠ ___MnQ___

International Time Zones. Add time zones to the map on page 115, and use it to help answer the following questions. Answer all questions as if time were stopped at 12:00 noon in Greenwich, England (along the prime meridian).

Need Help?
Check Out
Social Science Links at
www.SummerBridgeActivities.com

1. How many times zones are there? _____ Why do you think this number was chosen? _____

2. Time zones are calculated based on lines of _____ with _____ ° in each zone.

3. If time is calculated as hours added or subtracted from 12 noon at the prime meridian, what line of longitude would be at the center of the time zone containing the prime meridian? _____

4. On this map, assume it is 12 noon in Greenwich, England (Greenwich Mean Time is also called Zulu Time and is the reference point for all zones). What time is it in

   A. San Francisco, California, USA? _____   D. Mexico City, Mexico? _____

   B. Moscow, Russia? _____   E. Hobart, Tasmania, Australia? _____

   C. The Cook Islands? _____   F. Quebec, Canada? _____

5. Because the earth rotates from west to east, you subtract 1 hour for each 15° moving _____ and add 1 hour for each 15° moving _____.

6. 180° west or east of Greenwich is the International Date Line; the east is 12 hours ahead and the west is 12 hours behind, so by crossing the line there is a difference of _____ hours or _____. If you cross the line from west to east, you gain a day, but if you cross from east to west, you _____ a day.

7. The continental U.S., or lower 48, has _____ time zones. Canada has _____ time zones.

8. What time zone do you live in? _____ Which time zone is east of you? _____ Which time zone is west of you? _____

9. How many degrees of longitude are included in the complete time zone map of the earth? _____ °

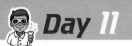

Light. Light travels in straight lines—until it runs into something. Consider each of these possibilities.

When light hits something opaque (which it can't pass through), we get a shadow. So, why do we have almost no shadow when the sun is high and there seems to be more light?

_____

_____

_____

_____

When light is reflected off a surface, it changes direction, but it still travels in straight lines.

Shine a flashlight on a handheld mirror. Move the mirror around.

What happens?

_____

_____

_____

_____

_____

When light passes through a substance (or what we call a medium), it can be refracted, or bent.

Fill a clear drinking glass with water. Place a pencil into the glass. Look at the pencil from several angles.

What do you see?

_____

_____

Writing a Business Letter. The style of a business letter is a little different from the style of a friendly letter. A business letter is somewhat more direct and more formal. Your letter will be a written record of your business transaction.

Write a business letter to address this situation: You ordered a necklace for your mother's birthday from Coco's Designer Jewelry, 1727 Monroe Street, Chicago, Illinois, 60625. In your order you had enclosed a check from your father for $31.98 including shipping charges. Your mother's birthday is only ten days away. The necklace has not arrived. Be sure to skip a line between each paragraph.

(your return address)
(your city, state, zip)
(today's date)

Coco's Designer Jewelry
1727 Monroe Street
Chicago, Illinois 60625

Attention: Mail Order Department

_____
_____
_____
_____
_____
_____
_____
_____
_____
_____
_____
_____
_____
_____
_____

(closing) _____

(signature)_____

 **Time Out:** Find an envelope, and address the envelope for this letter. Be sure to write the addresses in the proper places. Place capitals and punctuation marks where necessary.

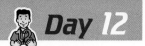
Relationship Among the Sides of Right Triangles. In a right triangle, the longest side is called the *hypotenuse*. The other sides are called *legs*. Square the numbers given on each side of the triangle. The sum of the squares of the legs is equal to the square of the hypotenuse. (The square of a number is the number times itself.)

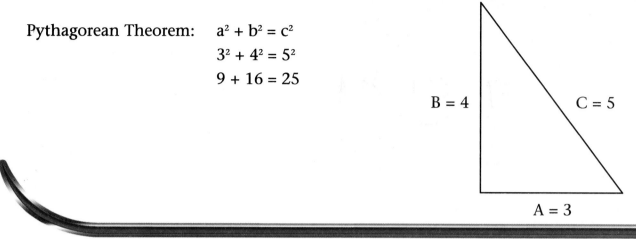

Pythagorean Theorem: $a^2 + b^2 = c^2$
$3^2 + 4^2 = 5^2$
$9 + 16 = 25$

B = 4   C = 5

A = 3

Write an equation to find the missing number; then solve the equation.

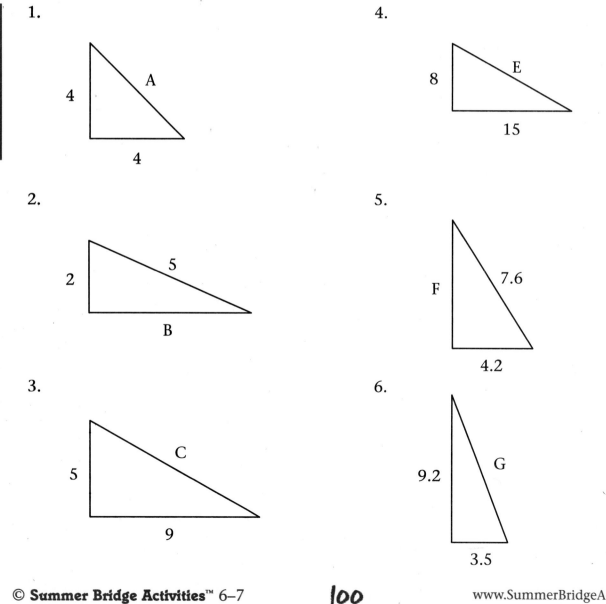

1.

4
A
4

2.

2
5
B

3.

5
C
9

4.

8
E
15

5.

F
7.6
4.2

6.

9.2
G
3.5

Many schools study state history in seventh grade. Get a head start by getting clued in to what makes your state great.

Caryle Calvin

What sort of state legislature do you have?

_____

_____

_____

Is it bicameral or unicameral?

_____

What district do you live in?

_____

Who is your state representative?

_____

What is your governor's name? _Mitch Daniels_

Where is he or she from? _IN,_

What political party does he or she belong to?

_____

What is the number one thing people come to your state to do or see?

_____ _Museums_ _____

DRAW YOUR STATE.

Draw a star for the capital.

Draw a house where you live.

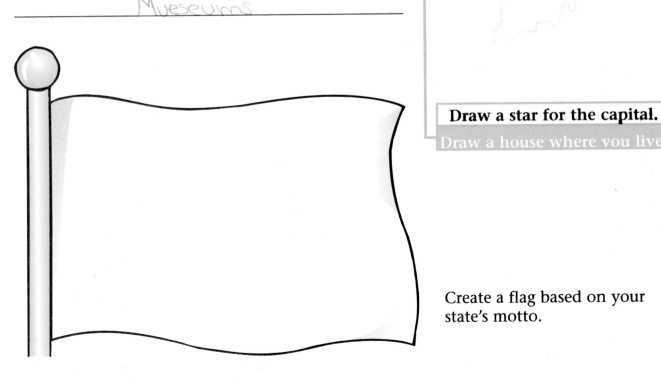

Create a flag based on your state's motto.

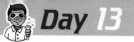

Day 13

Forces and Motion—Gravity. The earth's gravity pulls on every object at or near the earth's surface. This pull is always directed down toward the center, no matter where on the earth the object is located. The "power" of gravity's pull is the same for any object. Do you believe it?

Drop two objects of different size and weight. Hold one in each hand and drop them from the same height at the same time.

Record your results.

_____

_____

_____

_____

_____

_____

_____

Inertia. *Inertia* is the tendency of an object to stay at rest if at rest or to stay in motion if it is in motion—unless some other force influences the object.

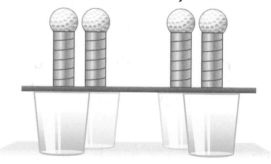

Materials:
4 cups, the same size
4 toilet paper tubes
4 golf balls
1 piece of cardboard
a long stick or ruler

Procedure:

1. Place the 4 cups on a flat surface such as the floor. Fill the cups half-full of water.
2. Place the flat piece of cardboard over the cups.
3. Place the 4 toilet paper tubes on the cardboard directly above the cups.
4. Place a golf ball on each of the toilet paper tubes.
5. With a long stick or ruler hit one edge of the cardboard solidly.

What were the results?

_____

_____

_____

_____

Identifying Dependent Clauses

> An *adjective clause* is a dependent clause that functions as an adjective modifying nouns or pronouns. An adjective clause usually begins with a relative pronoun: *who, whom, whose, whoever, which, what,* or *that.* An *adverb clause* is a dependent clause that functions as an adverb modifying verbs, adjectives, or other adverbs. An adverb clause usually begins with a *subordinating conjunction* such as *until, when, as, although,* or *if.* A *noun clause* is a dependent clause that functions as a noun. Some of the words that can introduce noun clauses are *that, why, what, which, whichever, who, whom, whoever, whomever,* and *whose.*

In each of the following sentences, underline the <u>dependent clause</u> and then indicate if it is an adjective clause (**ADJ**), an adverb clause (**ADV**), or a noun clause (**N**).

NEED HELP?
Check Out
Grammar Links at
www.SummerBridgeActivities.com

_____ 1. Joseph has a brown sweater that his grandmother knitted.

_____ 2. If you listen carefully to the directions, you should do well on this assignment.

_____ 3. I practiced my music lesson daily until I could play the selection perfectly.

_____ 4. The computer teacher already knows what the problem is.

_____ 5. The jewelry that my mother lost was worth a great deal of money.

_____ 6. George always eats hot dogs when he attends a basketball game.

_____ 7. Mr. Sanders read the announcement of the winners to whomever would listen.

_____ 8. Mr. Sanders's voice cracked as he read the winners.

Irregular Verbs. To form the past and past participle for *regular verbs*, add *-ed* or *-d.* The past and past participle of *irregular verbs* are formed in a variety of ways. The chart below shows the forms for some commonly used irregular verbs. Past participle forms are used with helping verbs such as *has, had, am, is, are, was,* and *were.*

PRESENT	PAST	PAST PARTICIPLE	PRESENT	PAST	PAST PARTICIPLE
begin	began	begun	leave	left	left
bring	brought	brought	lend	lent	lent
catch	caught	caught	throw	threw	thrown
drink	drank	drunk	know	knew	known
grow	grew	grown	draw	drew	drawn
show	showed	shown	sing	sang	sung

9. Ted Turner (threw, thrown) the first ball to start the baseball season.

10. Mrs. Parker said, "You may (begin, begun) the first part of the achievement test."

11. Have you (drank, drunk) all of the pink lemonade?

12. New students are (showed, shown) around the school by Mrs. Wright, our counselor.

13. My mother has (knew, known) our neighbors for about twelve years.

14. Several of my father's friends had (lend, lent) money to Melissa's family.

Statistics and Integers—Mean, Median, Mode, and Range. In a series of numbers, the difference between the greatest and smallest number is the *range*. The *median* is the middle number in an ordered set of numbers. The *mean* of the series of numbers is the average. *Mode* is a number in a set of data that appears more often than other numbers.

Give the mean, median, mode, and range for each series of numbers.

Series of numbers:

	Median	Mean	Mode	Range
1. 21, 19, 17, 11, 24, 16	18	18	18	13
2. 78, 45, 39, 62, 70	62	58.8	0	39
3. 28, 56, 44, 32, 52, 27	38	39.13	0	29
4. 130, 128, 180, 149	139.5	146.75	0	57

Integers. Whole numbers and their opposites are called *integers*. Numbers less than zero are called *negative numbers*; numbers greater than zero are called *positive numbers*. Zero is neither positive nor negative. Integers can be compared by comparing their position on a number line. The greater of two integers is always to the right. The integer to the left is the lesser integer. The sum of two positive integers is a positive integer. The sum of two negative integers is a negative integer. The sum of a positive integer and negative integer can be a positive integer, a negative integer, or zero.

Is the number an integer? Write Yes or No.

5. 8 Y   6. .07 N   7. 1/4 N   8. ⁻14 Y   9. π N   10. 0 Y   11. 5 Y

Write the opposite of the integer.

12. ⁻1 = 1   22. 6 ⁻6   32. 160 ⁻160   42. 199 ⁻199
13. 3 ⁻3   23. ⁻7 7   33. 240 ⁻240   43. 467 ⁻467
14. ⁻5 5   24. ⁻8 8   34. 9999 ⁻9999   44. 81 ⁻81
15. ⁻3 3   25. ⁻10 10   35. ⁻1000 1000   45. ⁻81 81
16. 5 ⁻5   26. ⁻30 30   36. ⁻873 873   46. ⁻240 240
17. 1 ⁻1   27. 45 ⁻45   37. 342 ⁻342   47. ⁻342 342
18. 7 ⁻7   28. 72 ⁻72   38. 16 ⁻16   48. 61 ⁻61
19. 0 0   29. ⁻17 17   39. ⁻72 72   49. ⁻100 100
20. ⁻6 6   30. 100 100   40. 249 ⁻249   50. 91 ⁻91
21. 8 ⁻8   31. ⁻200 200   41. 21 ⁻21   51. 82 ⁻82

More State Facts

Who are your state's senators?

_____

_____

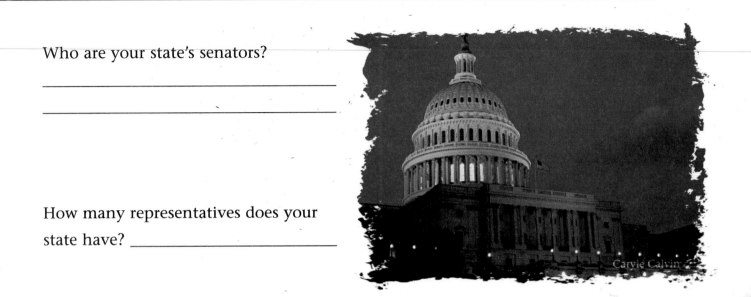

Caryle Calvin

How many representatives does your

state have? _____

Design a new license plate for your state. Use your state's nickname and include the year your state was admitted into the Union.

Indiana

500 RACE

DRAW AN OUTLINE OF EACH.

What is the largest county
or parish in your state?

_____

What is the smallest?

_____

Subtracting Integers. To subtract an integer, add its opposite. Solve the following problems.

1. 5 – 9
2. ‾3 – 8
3. 0 – 4
4. ‾2 – 0

5. 14 – ‾5
6. ‾9 – 12
7. 12 – 37
8. 3 – ‾7

9. ‾5 – ‾7
10. 0 – ‾7
11. ‾5 – ‾5
12. ‾17 – 9

13. ‾13 – ‾4
14. 42 – ‾15
15. ‾6 – 2
16. ‾4 – ‾10

Multiplying Integers. The product of two positive or two negative integers is positive. The product of a positive integer and a negative integer is negative. The product of any integer and zero is zero. Solve the following problems.

17. 2 × ‾1
18. ‾9 × 0
19. ‾8 × ‾9
20. ‾1 × 4
21. 10 × ‾2
22. 20 × 4
23. ‾15 × 3
24. ‾3 × ‾17

25. ‾6 × 6
26. ‾3 × 8
27. 5 × ‾9
28. 4 × 0
29. ‾7 × ‾11
30. 2 × ‾30
31. ‾6 × ‾13
32. 12 × ‾6

33. ‾4 × ‾3
34. 5 × 7
35. ‾8 × ‾5
36. 6 × ‾2
37. ‾13 × 2
38. ‾10 × ‾6
39. 5 × ‾12
40. ‾19 × 0

41. 4 × 10
42. ‾1 × ‾1
43. 5 × 5
44. ‾8 × ‾6
45. 9 × 7
46. ‾12 × ‾5
47. 4 × ‾7
48. 2 × 9

Dividing Integers. The quotient of two positive or two negative integers is positive. The quotient of a positive integer and a negative integer is negative. The quotient of zero divided by any other integer is zero. An integer cannot be divided by zero.

49. ‾18 ÷ 9
50. ‾24 ÷ ‾4
51. 81 ÷ ‾9
52. ‾26 ÷ 2
53. 16 ÷ ‾2
54. ‾64 ÷ 8

55. ‾7 ÷ 1
56. 84 ÷ ‾4
57. ‾30 ÷ ‾5
58. 42 ÷ 6
59. 0 ÷ ‾9
60. ‾46 ÷ ‾2

61. 56 ÷ ‾7
62. 6 ÷ ‾3
63. ‾28 ÷ 7
64. ‾48 ÷ 3
65. 24 ÷ 3
66. 72 ÷ ‾8

67. 9 ÷ 3
68. ‾8 ÷ 4
69. 18 ÷ 9
70. 36 ÷ 6
71. ‾36 ÷ 6
72. ‾15 ÷ ‾5

Page 3
1. S   2. F   3. S   4. S   5. F
6. F   7. S   8. F   9. S   10. S
11. advertisement 12. busiest   13. leisure
14. appreciate   15. changeable 16. athletic
17. protein   18. occasion   19. statement
20. druggist   21. classical   22. occupation

Page 4
1. one hundred eighty-seven thousand six hundred fifty-three
2. eighty-seven million four hundred sixty thousand thirty
3. two hundred twenty-two million three hundred thirty-three thousand one hundred eighty-nine
4. one billion two hundred thirty-four million five hundred sixty-seven thousand eight hundred ninety
5. five hundred forty-three billion two hundred one million sixty-five thousand four hundred eighty-three
6. 397,433   7. 509,877   8. 98,937   9. 8,650
10. 833,952 11. 108,270 12. 330.96 13. 5,391.405

Party Time
1. $20
2. Graduation: ($35 for spring, $40 for graduation)
3. Spring: more money on cups, plates, forks & napkins
4. Spring: about $70, Graduation: about $69
5. About $1

Page 5
1. E   2. G   3. C   4. I   5. B
6. A   7. H   8. F   9. D   10. J

Page 6

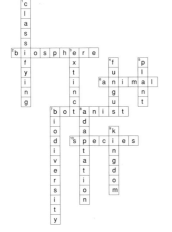

Page 7
1. C   2. B   3. A   4. B   5. D
6. A   7. C   8. B   9. D

Music and Dancing (Paragraph answers may vary.)

In the past, people in Europe and America danced their traditional folk dances at fairs, festivals, weddings, and celebrations. Folk dances are very old, and the steps have been passed down from parents to children for hundreds of years. Today they are mostly performed by dance groups in national costumes.

In other parts of the world, people have traditional dances that they perform at festivals or use to tell stories of their gods and heroes.

Page 8
1. 12
2. 4, 6, 8, 10, 12   3. 32, 48, 64, 80, 96
4. 14, 21, 28, 35, 42   5. 50, 75, 100, 125, 150
6. 20, 30, 40, 50, 60   7. 300, 450, 600, 750, 900
8. 10   9. 24   10. 35
11. 30   12. 24   13. 30
14. Yes   15. Yes   16. No   17. No   18. No
Challenge: Answers will vary. (about 20)

Page 9
1. Maine   2. Maryland   3. Rhode Island
4. New York   5. Pennsylvania   6. Vermont
7. Delaware   8. Massachusetts   9. Connecticut
10. New Hampshire   11. New Jersey
New England—Vermont, New Hampshire, Maine, Massachusetts, Rhode Island, Connecticut
Mid-Atlantic—New York, New Jersey, Pennsylvania, Maryland, Delaware
Northeast Region Word Search Answers:

```
k g k t f r g p s u c q o k
w k b t u c i t c e n n o c
t r r h o d e i s l a n d f
t o p z d n a l y r a m h y
d y o j e z y k j i y c s j
w w g d e l a w a r e u o i
f e a i n a v l y s n n e p
c n i i q v w g i i f o m u
m i l i r g n v e r m o n t
d a v n e w j e r s e y l v
n t i g f o h v y w z q d f
l n z n g y a c w t i r y y
e s t i e s u h c a s s a m
n e w h a m p s h i r e s m
```

Page 10
1. C   2. A   3. B   4. A
5. D   6. A   7. C   8. B
9. D   10. A   11. C   12. B

Page 11
Character Sketch: Answers will vary.
1. P boys run   2. C team plays
3. P Toni and sister ride   4. C band practices
5. S You were   6. P They have decided
7. P girls are going   8. S judging was held
9. P pennies are   10. C crowd stands

Page 12
1. Factors of 4: 1, 2, 4
   Factors of 8: 1, 2, 4, 8
   Common Factors: 1, 2, 4
   GCF: 4
2. Factors of 16: 1, 2, 4, 8, 16
   Factors of 20: 1, 2, 4, 5, 10, 20
   Common Factors: 1, 2, 4
   GCF: 4
3. 5   4. 12   5. 2   6. 3   7. 1
8. 4   9. 3   10. 5   11. 1
12. 6 players on 9 teams
13. 1, 2, 4, 8, 16, 31, 62, 124, 248

Answer Pages

Page 13

1. Texas, *Austin
2. Arkansas, *Little Rock
3. Louisiana, *Baton Rouge
4. Tennessee, *Nashville
5. Mississippi, *Jackson
6. Alabama, *Montgomery
7. Georgia, *Atlanta
8. Florida, *Tallahassee
9. South Carolina, *Columbia
10. North Carolina, *Raleigh
11. Kentucky, *Frankfort
12. Virginia, *Richmond
13. West Virginia, *Charleston
(from top to bottom) Mississippi, West Virginia, Georgia, Alabama, Virginia, Tennessee, South Carolina, North Carolina, Louisiana, Tennessee

Page 14

1. ocean
2. water
3. necessary
4. cycle
5. clouds
6. underneath
7. absorbs
8. sun
9. daylight
10. precipitation

```
y  p  a  p  s  d  l [n] i  m  g  c  u  r
y  o  m  j  f  c  b [u] u  x  v  l  z [u]
h  c  i  u  e  e  l [s] q [n] s  i  y [n]
q  b  r  t  n  k  u  y  o  b  d  s  f  d
[n  a  e  c  o] j  n [f  r  o  z  e  n] e
u  y  z  i  k  r  a  o  i  n  y  s  h  r
r  a  c  j  u  g  s  y  c  h  s  r  f  n
h  p  r  m  o  b  y  g  j  p  w  k  r  e
i  i [y  r  a  s  s  e  c  e  n] w  p  a
x [r  e  t  a  w] d  a  y  l  i  g  h  t
[n  o  i  t  a  t  i  p  i  c  e  r  p] h
g  j  g  h  j  q  i [s  d  u  o  l  c] h
d  t  t  p  o  h  n  h  e  j  t  p  w  p
g [e  l  c  y  c] h  s  s  k  m  v  a  o
```

Page 15

1. bored
2. herd
3. They're
4. allowed
5. passed
6. suite, sweet
7. whether, weather
8. principal, principle
9. Write
10. capital
11. from her new boyfriend
12. about the Oregon Trail
13. on vacation to the Grand Canyon
14. for the problems on this test
15. behind us
16. underneath your coat
17. in the morning with breakfast with lunch
18. around the corner across the street from the dry cleaners

Page 16

1. $\frac{3}{36}$
2. $\frac{1}{3}$
3. $\frac{9}{12}$
4. $\frac{4}{4}$
5. $\frac{4}{4}$
6. $\frac{8}{36}$
7. $\frac{7}{14}$
8. $\frac{1}{9}$
9. $\frac{14}{12}$
10. $\frac{39}{45}$
11. $\frac{4}{32}$
12. $\frac{4}{20}$
13. $\frac{8}{12}$
14. $\frac{2}{3}$
15. $\frac{35}{105}$
16. $\frac{6}{10} = \frac{3}{5}$
17. $\frac{3}{12} = \frac{1}{4}$
18. $\frac{7}{8} = \frac{28}{32}$
19. $\frac{13}{26} = \frac{1}{2}$
20. $\frac{11}{20} = \frac{22}{40}$
21. $\frac{3}{8} = \frac{18}{48}$
22. $\frac{2}{9} = \frac{4}{18}$
23. $\frac{13}{14} = \frac{26}{28}$
24. $\frac{11}{15} = \frac{33}{45}$

Page 17

1. OK
2. IA
3. MI
4. KS
5. WI
6. SD
7. MN
8. OH
9. ND
10. MO
11. NE

1. North Dakota, *Bismarck
2. South Dakota, *Pierre
3. Nebraska, *Lincoln
4. Kansas, *Topeka
5. Oklahoma, *Oklahoma City
6. Minnesota, *St. Paul
7. Iowa, *Des Moines
8. Missouri, *Jefferson City
9. Wisconsin, *Madison
10. Illinois, *Springfield
11. Indiana, *Indianapolis
12. Ohio, *Columbus
13. Michigan, *Lansing

Page 19

1. C
2. S
3. C
4. S
5. C
6. S
7. S
8. C
9. C
10. S
11. whom
12. who
13. Whom
14. who
15. who
16. whom
17. whom
18. who
19. whom
20. who

Page 20

1. 36/36, equivalent
2. 105/60, not equivalent
3. 12/18, not equivalent
4. 180/180, equivalent
5. 315/280, not equivalent
6. 360/360, equivalent
7. $\frac{10}{12}, \frac{11}{12}$
8. $\frac{5}{15}, \frac{6}{15}$
9. $\frac{5}{20}, \frac{6}{20}$
10. $\frac{12}{33}, \frac{3}{33}$
11. $\frac{3}{30}, \frac{8}{30}$
12. $\frac{3}{9}, \frac{2}{9}$
13. $\frac{27}{45}, \frac{20}{45}$
14. $\frac{9}{63}, \frac{35}{63}$
15. $\frac{7}{7} > \frac{4}{7}$
16. $\frac{7}{8} > \frac{3}{4}$
17. $\frac{1}{3} < \frac{7}{12}$
18. $\frac{1}{2} < \frac{5}{8}$

Page 21

Capitals (top to bottom) 11, 7, 5, 13, 12, 3, 8, 2, 4, 1, 9, 6, 10
Cities (top to bottom) 13, 10, 1, 5, 2, 3, 6, 7, 8, 12, 4, 9, 11

Page 23

Paragraph: Answer will vary.
1. really likes
2. always goes
3. never gives
4. quickly burned
5. very tired
6. hard studied
7. quickly work
8. too tired
9. Suddenly heard
10. easily worked

Page 24

1. $\frac{1}{7} < \frac{4}{7}, \frac{2}{7} < \frac{4}{7}$
2. $\frac{3}{8} < \frac{3}{4}, \frac{5}{8} < \frac{3}{4}$
3. $\frac{1}{3} > \frac{1}{12}, \frac{1}{3} < \frac{5}{12}$
4. $\frac{1}{2} > \frac{1}{8}, \frac{1}{2} > \frac{3}{8}$
5. $\frac{16}{24}$, on Internet, $\frac{21}{24}$ watching TV
6. $\frac{3}{12}$ Wednesday, $\frac{4}{12}$ Friday
7. $\frac{14}{35}$ Friday, $\frac{15}{35}$ Saturday

1. $\frac{1}{3}$
2. $\frac{1}{5}$
3. $\frac{1}{4}$
4. $\frac{1}{4}$
5. $\frac{1}{2}$
6. $\frac{2}{3}$
7. $\frac{7}{10}$
8. $\frac{5}{18}$
9. $\frac{2}{5}$
10. $\frac{9}{10}$
11. $\frac{29}{36}$
12. $\frac{1}{19}$

Page 25

Branch 1. Executive, 2. Legislative, 3. Judicial
Branch—Executive. Who? President. What? Carry out and enforce laws. How? Commander in Chief of Armed Forces, Cabinet and Executive Staff.
Branch—Legislative. Who? Congress (Senate & House of Representatives). What? Make the laws. How? Laws passed by majority vote.
Branch—Judicial. Who? Supreme Court and Lower Courts. What? Interpret or explain laws. How? Hears and makes decisions about cases involving questions about the Constitution, federal laws, treaties, and shipping.

Answer Pages

Page 27
1. Carla
2. report
3. libraries
4. Sweden
5. students
6. coats
7. students
8. heartbeat
9. George
10. Sara and Juanita

The following adjectives are circled:
11. several
12. red, yellow, blue
13. those, priceless
14. historical
15. contest, green
16. bright, unusual
17. These, science, best
18. quiet, studious
19. beautiful, clever
20. five, hard, steady

Page 28
1. $\frac{5}{2}$
2. $\frac{24}{5}$
3. $\frac{19}{5}$
4. $\frac{21}{5}$
5. $\frac{17}{5}$
6. $\frac{8}{3}$
7. $\frac{19}{3}$
8. $\frac{61}{9}$
9. $1\frac{5}{6}$
10. $1\frac{6}{11}$
11. $2\frac{1}{7}$
12. $4\frac{1}{8}$
13. $5\frac{1}{5}$
14. 5
15. $8\frac{1}{3}$
16. $8\frac{8}{9}$
17. $4\frac{1}{3}$
18. $3\frac{1}{3}$
19. $4\frac{3}{4}$
20. $6\frac{1}{2}$
21. 3 boxes
22. $5\frac{1}{3}$ servings

Page 29
1. Belize, *Belmopan
2. Guatemala, *Guatemala City
3. Honduras, *Tegucigalpa
4. El Salvador, *San Salvador
5. Nicaragua, *Managua
6. Costa Rica, *San Jose
7. Panama, *Panama City

Page 30
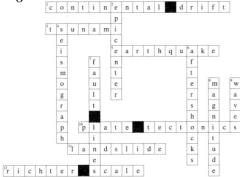

Page 31
1. but
2. Because, or
3. or
4. Either, or
5. When
6. Neither, nor
7. and
8. Although
9. but
10. since
11. receives
12. makes
13. do
14. is
15. were
16. has
17. look
18. are
19. practice
20. share

Page 32
1. .4
2. .225
3. .0875
4. $.\overline{5}$
5. $.3\overline{18}$
6. 4.07
7. 9.125
8. 4.625
9. .18
10. .025
11. $.\overline{3}$
12. $.58\overline{3}$
13. .385
14. 8.67
15. 1.375
16. 5.68

17. .02
18. .375
19. .453
20. $.0\overline{6}$
21. .568
22. 7.87
23. 7.4
24. $3.\overline{6}$
25. .75
26. .64
27. $.8\overline{2}$
28. $.8\overline{3}$
Time Out: The steak cost 86¢ more per pound.

Page 35
1. Bahamas Islands
2. Windward
3. Caribbean Sea
4. Straits of Florida
5. Hispaniola
6. Caribbean
7. European
8. Dutch
9. Rimland
10. Poverty

Page 37 Answers may vary.
1. Whew
2. Goodness
3. Wow
4. Hurrah
5. Oh or My
6. Gosh
7. Alas
8. Ugh
9. Well
10. My or Oh
11. Ouch
12. Gracious
13. Your
14. hers
15. mine
16. my
17. its
18. ours
19. Their
20. your

```
v z w e h w n e h h
i g o o d n e s s g
t i w h s o g f u
d e k z l m m r h d
t a l a s x h a n
m o t w o w c r m
b x w h o c u i r s
u l k s f r o u d
h a u l l e w u h k
o e w z m y k s i m
```

Page 38
1. $\frac{3}{4}$
2. $1\frac{1}{9}$
3. $\frac{1}{2}$
4. $\frac{3}{10}$
5. $\frac{9}{16}$
6. $\frac{3}{4}$
7. $1\frac{2}{15}$
8. $\frac{2}{5}$
9. $\frac{2}{9}$
10. $\frac{15}{19}$
11. $\frac{9}{11}$
12. 1
13. $\frac{1}{3}$
14. $\frac{1}{8}$
15. $1\frac{1}{5}$
16. $\frac{3}{10}$
17. $1\frac{13}{28}$
18. $1\frac{5}{12}$
19. $\frac{1}{3}$
20. $\frac{1}{20}$
21. $1\frac{1}{12}$

Page 39
1. Venezuela, *Caracas
2. Colombia, *Bogota
3. Ecuador, *Quito
4. Peru, *Lima
5. Guyana, *Georgetown
6. Suriname, *Paramaribo
7. French Guiana, *Cayenne
8. Brazil, *Brasilia
9. Bolivia, *La Paz and Sucre
10. Chile, *Santiago
11. Argentina, *Buenos Aires
12. Paraguay, *Asunción
13. Uruguay, *Montevideo
    Ecuador, Colombia, Brazil
    Chile
    French Guiana
    Boliva

Page 40
1. crust
2. Mohorovicic discontinuity
3. lithosphere
4. mantle
5. asthenosphere
6. core
7. outer core
8. inner core
9. Gutenberg discontinuity

Page 41
1. B
2. C
3. A
4. D
5. B
6. C
7. A
8. A

Page 42
1. $8\frac{3}{20}$
2. $8\frac{2}{5}$
3. $4\frac{1}{4}$
4. $11\frac{1}{8}$
5. $8\frac{3}{5}$
6. $2\frac{17}{48}$
7. $4\frac{1}{15}$
8. $16\frac{1}{10}$
9. $7\frac{7}{24}$

Answer Pages

Page 43 Answers will vary.

Page 45
1. good
2. polite
3. easily
4. interesting
5. Surely
6. hard
7. slowly
8. beautiful
9. thoroughly
10. badly
11. lay
12. sat
13. lain
14. rises
15. risen
16. sit
17. laid
18. set
19. laid
20. raised

Page 46
1. $\frac{7}{24}$
2. $\frac{3}{8}$
3. $\frac{5}{18}$
4. $\frac{1}{2}$
5. $\frac{1}{3}$
6. $\frac{8}{45}$
7. $\frac{5}{28}$
8. $\frac{2}{3}$
9. $\frac{3}{16}$
10. $\frac{1}{5}$
11. $\frac{3}{10}$
12. $\frac{5}{24}$
13. $\frac{1}{12}$
14. $\frac{1}{2}$
15. $\frac{28}{33}$

Page 47 • Western Europe
1. 5
2. Liechtenstein
3. 17
4. Sweden
5. 9
6. 25
7. 6
8. 2
9. 15
10. Switzerland

Page 49
1. ate, direct object
2. offered, indirect object
3. wrote, direct object
4. bought, indirect object
5. fed, indirect object
6. gave, indirect object
7. told, direct object
8. gave, direct object
9. feeds, indirect object
10. sold, direct object
11. 2
12. 8
13. 3
14. 5
15. 1
16. 7
17. 4
18. 6
19. 1
20. 6
21. 3
22. 2
23. 7
24. 4

Page 50
1. $12\frac{1}{4}$
2. $15\frac{1}{2}$
3. $17\frac{19}{24}$
4. $15\frac{41}{42}$
5. 19
6. $10\frac{2}{5}$
7. $\frac{5}{3}$
8. $\frac{8}{4}$
9. $\frac{11}{7}$
10. $\frac{12}{6}$
11. $\frac{9}{5}$
12. $\frac{4}{3}$
13. $\frac{1}{8}$
14. $\frac{11}{8}$
15. $\frac{21}{18}$
16. $\frac{1}{25}$
17. $\frac{1}{142}$
18. $\frac{7}{4}$
19. $\frac{14}{13}$
20. $\frac{25}{6}$
21. $\frac{1}{32}$
22. $\frac{1}{16}$

Page 51

29	36
34	40
48	38
32	42

Page 53 Paragraphs will vary.

August 10, 2000

Dear Aunt Emily and Uncle Bob,

Thank you so much for my twelfth birthday party. All of my friends really enjoyed the pizza and skating party at Sal's Skating Palace.

Mom and Dad must have told you that I wanted a pizza and skating party. I have heard from almost everyone who attended. What a great time!

As soon as the pictures are developed, Mom and I will send you some of the prints. I can't wait to see them!

Thanks again for such a wonderful birthday party.

Love,
Marsha

Page 54
1. $1\frac{1}{2}$
2. $1\frac{3}{7}$
3. $6\frac{2}{9}$
4. $1\frac{1}{8}$
5. $\frac{12}{19}$
6. $1\frac{3}{5}$
7. $\frac{15}{16}$
8. $\frac{2}{3}$
9. $1\frac{1}{3}$
10. $1\frac{19}{392}$
11. $\frac{3}{20}$
12. $\frac{3}{4}$
13. $1\frac{43}{56} < 4\frac{2}{15}$
14. $5\frac{5}{8} > 2\frac{19}{24}$
15. $12\frac{15}{32} > 9\frac{7}{12}$
16. $6\frac{13}{34} < 51\frac{1}{3}$

Page 55

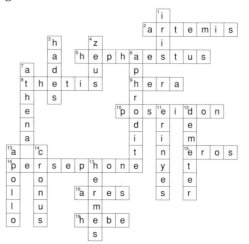

Page 57 Answers will vary.

Page 58
1. P = $1\frac{2}{3}$ yards
2. $2.25
3. $3.90
4. (a) $1\frac{1}{2}$ gallons; (b) no; (c) 2 gallons; (d) $10\frac{1}{2}$ gallons
5. $\frac{5}{12}$
6. $\frac{1}{8}$

Page 59 (from top to bottom)
H, C, J, M, E, A, G, B, L, I, D, K, N, F

Page 61
1. happier, happiest
2. more beautiful, most beautiful
3. weaker, weakest
4. more talented, most talented
5. louder, loudest
6. more slowly, most slowly
7. farther, farthest
8. more quietly, most quietly
9. more politely, most politely
10. higher, highest
11. funniest
12. extremely
13. more carefully
14. sure
15. good
16. better
17. more attentively
18. warmer
19. more expensive
20. taller
21. greatest
22. bigger
23. fastest
24. oldest
25. least

Page 62
1. $\frac{154}{167}$
2. $1\frac{21}{37}$
3. $1\frac{13}{154}$
4. $\frac{29}{77}$
5. $\frac{37}{416}$
6. $\frac{29}{208}$
7. $19\frac{8}{43}$
8. $\frac{43}{825}$
9. $\frac{1}{5}$
10. $\frac{5}{42}$
11. $\frac{7}{100}$
12. 20

Page 63 • Answers will vary. Some examples:

Page — began in household of lord at age 7; learned to ride a horse; received religious training and instruction on table manners, hunting, and dancing

Squire — became assistant to a knight at age 12–13; looked after knight's weapons and armor; became skilled in their use; served knight his meals; followed him into battle (only one squire was allowed to assist in tournaments); older squires enter tournaments, went through "ordeal" right before becoming an accolade

Knight sworn to uphold code of chivalry; fought on horseback; owned expensive armor, weapons, and horses; owned land and castles; fought in the Crusades

Page 65
1. The Grand Canyon is one of the world's natural wonders.
2. Arizona 3. 1 day 4. C 5. D
6. You get the best appreciation of it. 7. 8,000 ft.

Page 66
A. 3 B. 4 C. 20 D. 37
1. 75¢ each
2. 10¢ each
3. $7.50/bouquet
4. 40 nails/box
5. $320.00/camera
Part-time Earnings: 2 days = $97.00 5 days = $242.50
10 days = $485.00
Time Out: 10 minutes/section

Page 67
KUSH Where? South of Egypt. When? 750 B.C.–A.D. 150. History? Dominated by Egypt; learned much of their culture. Resources? Iron tools, gold objects. Accomplishments? Defeated Egypt; was a center of culture.
ETHIOPIA Where? Between the Nile River and the Red Sea. When? About A.D. 325 to present. History? Rich and powerful trade center; King Ezana became a Christian in A.D. 324. Resources? Location between the Red Sea and the African interior. Accomplishments? Destroyed Meroe; its major trade city Axum remained Christian and undefeated.
MALI Where? West Africa on Senegal and West Niger Rivers. When? A.D. 1235–1468. History? Emerged after fall of Ghana trade and learning center, Timbuktu. Resources? Gold, salt for trade. Accomplishments? A learned, rich, and generous city; they were great traders.
SONGHAI Where? West African Niger River. When? About A.D. 1464–1591. History? Controlled West Africa after conquering Mali. Resources? Salt, trading center at Timbuktu. Accomplishments? Great trade center; center of commerce Tarhaza where houses were built of salt slabs.

Page 69
I. The pioneers
A. Conquering the wilderness
B. Establishing the frontier
II. Moving westward
A. Crossing the Appalachians
B. How pioneers traveled
III. A pioneer settlement
A. A pioneer home
B. Education and religion
C. Law and order
D. Social activities
E. Indian attacks
IV. Crossing the plains
A. The wagon trail
B. Life on the trail

Page 70
1. yes 2. no 3. no 4. no 5. yes 6. no
7. 7:12 or $\frac{7}{12}$ 8. 3:5 or $\frac{3}{5}$ 9. 30:1 or $\frac{30}{1}$
10. 4:1 or $\frac{4}{1}$ 11. 20:3 or $\frac{20}{3}$ 12. 13:3 or $\frac{13}{3}$
13. p = 2 14. a = 60 15. x = 10
16. x = 6 17. k = 4.5 18. x = 14

Page 71
1. L 2. F 3. N 4. B
5. R 6. J 7. D 8. S
9. P 10. C 11. M 12. G
13. Q 14. A 15. I 16. T
17. O 18. E 19. K 20. H
Time Out: Answers will vary.

Page 72
Geologists; plates; trench; mantle; magma; volcanoes; mountain; (in any order) cinder, shield, composite; reservoir, conduit, craters, fissures, Pacific, Igneous, molten, lava

Page 73
1. D 2. A 3. C 4. B 5. A 6. C
7. B 8. D 9. A 10. B 11. D 12. B
13. D 14. A 15. C 16. B 17. A 18. D
19. A 20. C

Page 74
1. n = 20 2. a = 2 3. n = 18 4. a = 15
5. a = 90 6. a = 9 7. x = 8 8. x = 30
9. x = 51 10. n = 9 11. y = 23 12. p = 52
13. 18 14. $15.39 15. 35, 24, no
16. 60, 60, yes 17. 24, 24 yes

Page 77
1. artists 2. scientists
3. writers 4. religious reformers/leaders
5. queens 6. Italian city-states
7. inventors 8. kings/absolute monarchs
9. poets 10. composers

Page 78
1. F 2. E 3. I 4. D 5. A 6. C
7. H 8. B 9. G

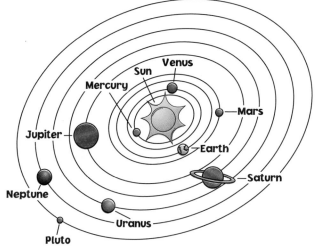

Page 79

1. D	2. B	3. A	4. C	5. A	6. C
7. D	8. B	9. A	10. B	11. A	12. C
13. D	14. B	15. B	16. C	17. B	18. A
19. D	20. A				

Page 80

1. 13   2. 27   3. 9   4. 40, $\frac{2}{5}$

5. 50, $\frac{1}{2}$ 6. 90, $\frac{9}{10}$ 7. 85, $\frac{17}{20}$ 8. 12, $\frac{3}{25}$

9. 4, $\frac{1}{25}$ 10. 67%   11. 7%   12. 90%

Page 81

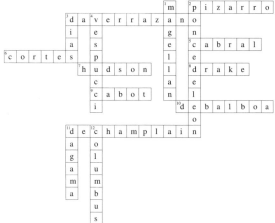

Page 82

1. macronucleus   2. food vacuoles, water vacuoles
3. cilia   4. micronucleus   5. contractile vacuole
cilia—movement; water vacuole—store water;
food vacuole—store food; large nucleus—controls
paramecium; small nucleus—aids in reproduction;
contractile vacuole—gets rid of waste

Page 83

1. West Palm Street, Houston Mill Road
2. Salt Lake City, Utah
3. Rome, Venice, Italy
4. Nile River, Mediterranean Sea
5. Washington, D.C., Lincoln Memorial
6. Mount Logan, Canada
7. Asia

Page 84

1. 65%	2. 7%	3. 3%	4. 12%	5. 72%
6. 41%	7. 29%	8. 50%	9. 84%	10. 0.34
11. 0.58	12. 0.13	13. 0.91	14. 0.08	15. 0.16

Page 85 • Sample Answers:

1. Effect: Improved technology, growth of the working middle class, growth of cities
2. Effect: French Revolution
3. Cause: Peter the Great traveled incognito through Europe and became convinced that Russia was backward in technical and social development.
4. Effect: Rise of Lenin and the Communist Revolution
5. Cause: Stalin began a series of "5 Year Plans" to modernize Russia.

6. Effect: World War I
7. Cause: Germans blame the Treaty of Versailles and economic depression for their troubles.
8. Effect: Germany and the Axis Powers lose World War II.
9. Cause: Allied leaders meet at Yalta to plan Europe's future.

Page 86

Column one:	A	B	C	D	E	F	G	H	I
Column two:	C	F	D	A	G	H	I	E	B
Column three:	G	F	A	I	H	B	D	C	E

Page 87

1. F	2. S	3. S	4. F	5. S
6. S	7. F	8. F	9. F	10. S

11. Dickens's   12. guardsmen's   13. newspapers'
14. year's   15. Margaret's   16. Harrison's
17. sister's   18. characters'   19. teachers'
20. nations'   21. Harris's   22. Vincent's
23. children's   24. referee's   25. governor's

Page 88

1. $\frac{1}{12}$ 2. $\frac{1}{6}$ 3. $\frac{1}{4}$ 4. $\frac{1}{2}$ 5. $\frac{3}{8}$ 6. $\frac{1}{4}$ 7. $\frac{1}{2}$ 8. $\frac{1}{2}$
9. $\frac{2}{9}$ 10. $\frac{5}{9}$ 11. $\frac{1}{9}$ 12. 0 13. $\frac{1}{4}$ 14. $\frac{7}{12}$ 15. $\frac{1}{6}$ 16. 0

Page 89 • From left to right:

17. 2590 B.C.	1. 1500 B.C.	9. 1200 B.C.
6. 776 B.C.	11. 753 B.C.	5. 202 B.C.
18. 0	10. A.D. 641	2. A.D. 750
19. A.D. 790	8. A.D. 1175	12. A.D. 1200
7. A.D. 1614	20. A.D. 1760	3. A.D. 1761
14. A.D. 1776	13. A.D. 1789	16. A.D. 1863
4. A.D. 1917	15. A.D. 1989	

Page 90

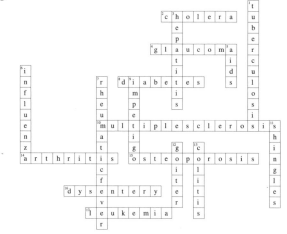

Page 91 • Proofreading:

Although Elvis Aaron Presley did not invent rock 'n' roll, he did more than anyone to popularize it. He was rock's most powerful performer. From the mid-50s, the "King's" vocal mannerism, sideburns, and attitude made him an international hero of the young.

During his lifetime, Elvis sold more than four hundred million records. He had forty-five golden hit records. Elvis also appeared in thirty-two movies.

When Presley died on August 16, 1977, at the age of forty-two, many mourners journeyed to Memphis, Tennessee, Presley's home, to pay their last respects. Elvis left behind an almost immeasurable influence on popular music.

Add commas after the following:
1. studies, believe   2. me, Ralph   3. lunch
4. said, record   5. Harrison   6. story
7. test   8. This, suppose   9. Blake   10. Plains

Page 92
1. V = 1,134 cm³   2. V = 720 cm³   3. V = 264 m³
4. V = 50.4 cm³   5. V = 180 m³   6. V = 197.392 cm³

Page 93
1. Greenland, Godthåb (Nuuk)   2. Canada, Ottawa
3. U.S., Washington, D.C.   4. Mexico, Mexico City
5. Guatemala, Guatemala City   6. Belize, Belmopan
7. Honduras, Tegucigalpa   8. El Salvador, San Salvador
9. Nicaragua, Managua   10. Costa Rica, San José
11. Panama, Panama City
12. Trinidad and Tobago, Port-of-Spain
13. Puerto Rico, San Juan   14. Hispaniola
15. Jamaica, Kingston   16. Cuba, Havana
17. Bahamas, Nassau   18. Gulf of Mexico
19. Atlantic Ocean   20. Hudson Bay
21. Arctic Ocean   22. Pacific Ocean
23. Colorado River   24. Mississippi River
25. Mackenzie River

Page 94
1. cell membrane   2. nucleus   3. vacuole
4. cytoplasm 5. nucleus   6. chloroplast 7. cell wall

Page 95
1. Its   2. There   3. you're   4. Whose   5. to
6. won   7. your   8. They're 9. one   10. two

Page 96
1. C   2. CBD   3. CDB   4. $\overline{DC}$ 5. $\overline{MQ}$
6. $\overline{ML}$ 7. $\overline{MN}$ 8. MQN   9. NMQ   10. MNQ

Page 97
1. 24. One zone for each hour in the day. The amount
   of time it takes the earth to rotate on its axis.
2. longitude, 15° 3. 0°
4. A. 4 a.m. B. 3 p.m. C. 2 a.m. D. 6 a.m. E. 11 p.m.
   F. 7 a.m.   5. west, east   6. 24, 1 day, lose
7. 4, 5   8. Answers will vary. 9. 360°

Page 98
1. Because a shadow is also dependent on the angle of
   the light source compared to the opaque object.
2. When a ray of light strikes a mirror at a slant or
   angle, the ray is reflected at a slant, or angle, in
   another direction.
3. When light rays pass at a slant, or angle, from one
   transparent material (such as air) into another transparent material (such as water), the light rays are
   bent, or refracted, so that they travel in a different
   direction. This makes the pencil look bent.

Page 100
1. $4^2 + 4^2 = A^2$, A = 5.65685   2. $B^2 = 5^2 - 2^2$, B = 4.58
3. $5^2 + 9^2 = C^2$, C = 10.2956   4. $8^2 + 15^2 = E^2$, E = 17
5. $F^2 = 7.6^2 - 4.2^2$, F = 6.334 6. $9.2^2 + 3.5^2 = G^2$, G= 9.843

Page 102
Both objects fall at the same rate and should hit the floor
at the same time. Objects may not hit the floor at the same
time if moved upon by another force. For example: If a
feather or paper were used, the air would slow the descent.

The golf balls should have splashed into the cups. The
cups are held in place by the water, so the friction of the
cardboard does not affect them. The cardboard is affected
by another object (the ruler). The toilet paper tubes slide
with the cardboard due to friction. The golf balls are
pulled toward the glasses by gravity.

Page 103
1. ADJ that his grandmother knitted
2. ADV If you listen carefully to the directions
3. ADV until I could play the selection perfectly
4. N what the problem is
5. ADJ that my mother lost
6. ADV when he attends a basketball game
7. N whomever would listen
8. ADV as he read the winners
9. threw   10. begin   11. drunk
12. shown   13. known   14. lent

Page 104
1. median = 18 mean = 18 mode = no mode range = 13
2. median = 62 mean = 58.8 mode = no mode range = 39
3. median = 38 mean = 39.83 mode = no mode range = 29
4. median = 139.5 mean = 146.75 mode = no mode range = 52
5. Yes   6. No   7. No   8. Yes   9. No
10. Yes   11. Yes   12. 1   13. -3   14. 5
15. 3   16. -5   17. -1   18. -7   19. 0
20. 6   21. -8   22. -6   23. 7   24. 8
25. 10   26. 30   27. -45   28. -72   29. 17
30. -100   31. 200   32. -160   33. -240   34. -9999
35. 1000   36. 873   37. -342   38. -16   39. 72
40. -249   41. -21   42. -199   43. -467   44. -81
45. 81   46. 240   47. 342   48. -61   49. 100
50. -91   51. -82

Page 106
1. -4   2. -11   3. -4   4. -2   5. 19
6. -21   7. -25   8. 10   9. 2   10. 7
11. 0   12. -26   13. -9   14. 57   15. -8
16. 6   17. -2   18. 0   19. 72   20. -4
21. -20   22. 80   23. -45   24. 51   25. -36
26. -24   27. -45   28. 0   29. 77   30. -60
31. 78   32. -72   33. 12   34. 35   35. 40
36. -12   37. -26   38. 60   39. -60   40. 0
41. 40   42. 1   43. 25   44. 48   45. 63
46. 60   47. -28   48. 18   49. -2   50. 6
51. -9   52. -13   53. -8   54. -8   55. -7
56. -21   57. 6   58. 7   59. 0   60. 23
61. -8   62. -2   63. -4   64. -16   65. 8
66. -9   67. 3   68. -2   69. 2   70. 6
71. -6   72. 3

Page 5 Global Grid Reference

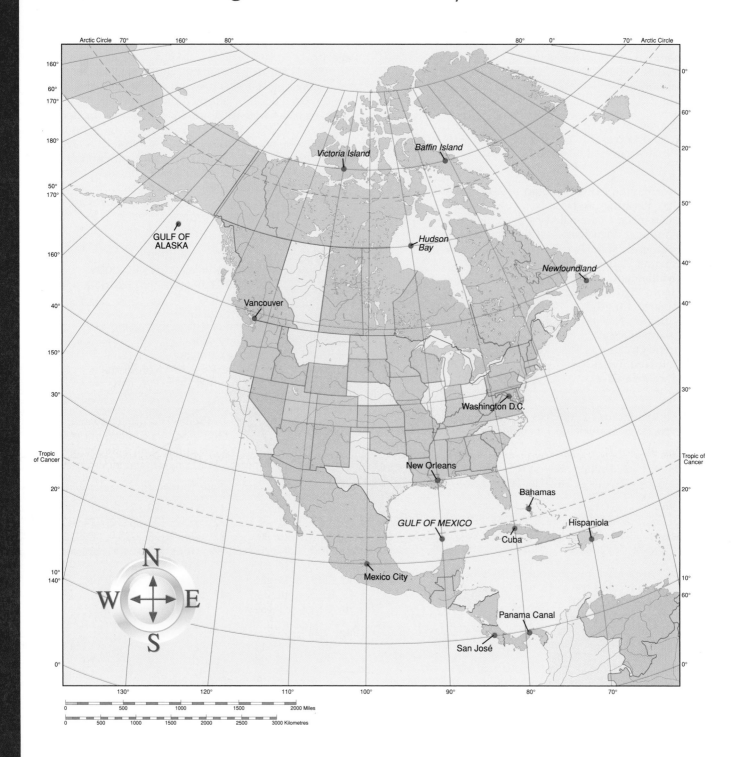

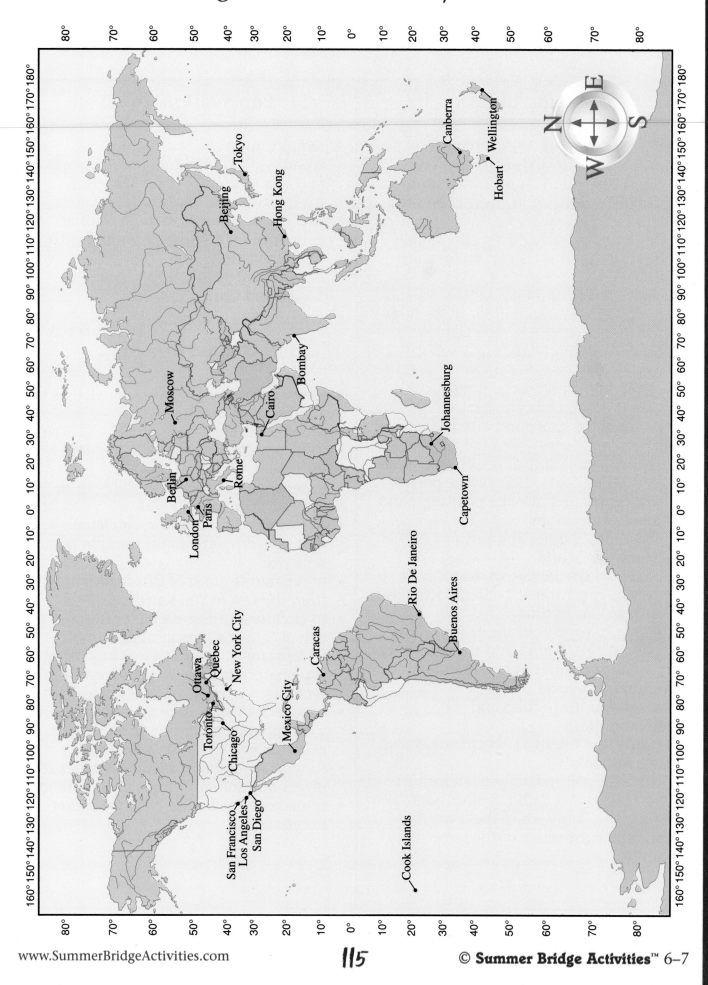

QUICK REFERENCE CHART

CAPITALIZATION AND PUNCTUATION GUIDE

Capitalize:

- the first word of every sentence
- proper nouns and proper adjectives
- the first word in a direct quotation
- the first word in the greeting and the closing of a letter
- names of people and also the initials or abbreviations that stand for those names
- titles used with names of persons and abbreviations standing for those titles
- the first letter of the first, last, and other important words in a title
- names of the days of the week, months of the year, and special holidays
- names of languages, races, nationalities, religions, and proper adjectives formed from them
- the first word and all important words in titles of books, periodicals, poems, stories, articles, movies, paintings, and other works of art
- geographic names and sections of the country or world
- names of special events, historical events, government bodies, documents, and periods of time
- names of organizations, institutions, associations, teams, and their members
- names of businesses and brand names of their products
- abbreviations of titles and organizations
- words that refer to a specific deity and sacred books
- words denoting family relationships such as *mother, father, brother, aunt, uncle,* etc., only when these words stand for the name of the same individual

Punctuation Rules:

A period is used . . .
- at the end of a declarative sentence as well as a mild imperative sentence
- after initials and abbreviations
- after numbers and letters in outlines
- only once for a sentence ending with an abbreviation
- as a decimal point and to separate dollars and cents

A comma is used ...

- to separate words, phrases, or clauses in a series (at least three items)
- to set off a direct quotation
- to separate the names of a city and state in an address
- to separate the month and day from the year in a date
- to set off a word, phrase, or clause that interrupts the main thought of a sentence
- to separate a noun of direct address from the rest of the sentence
- to enclose a title, a name, or initials which follow a person's last name
- to separate an appositive or any other explanatory phrase from the rest of the sentence
- to separate two independent clauses in a compound sentence joined by such words as *but, or, for, so, yet*
- to separate digits in a number to set off places of hundreds, thousands, millions
- to make the meaning clear whenever necessary

QUICK REFERENCE CHART

PUNCTUATION GUIDE

A semicolon is used ...

- to separate two independent clauses very close in meaning but not joined by *and, but, or, nor, for,* or *yet*
- to separate groups of words or phrases which already contain commas
- to connect two independent clauses when the second clause begins with a conjunctive adverb such as *however, therefore,* or *then*

A colon is used ...

- after the greeting of a formal letter
- before a list of items or details, especially after expressions such as *as follows* and *the following*
- before a long, formal statement or quotation
- between independent clauses when the second clause explains the first clause
- between the parts of a number which indicate time

Parentheses are used ...

- to enclose incidental explanatory matter which is added to a sentence but is not considered of major importance
- to enclose a question mark after a date or statement to show some doubt

Dashes are used ...

- to indicate an abrupt break in thought in the sentence
- to mean *namely, in other words, that is,* etc., before an explanation

A hyphen is used ...

- to divide a word at the end of a line (divide only between syllables)
- to join the words in compound numbers from twenty-one to ninety-nine and with fractions used as adjectives
- with the prefixes *ex-, self-, all-,* with the suffix *-elect,* and with all prefixes before a proper noun or proper adjective
- to prevent confusion or awkwardness

A question mark is used ...

- at the end of a direct question (an interrogative sentence)
- inside quotation marks when the quotation is a question

An exclamation mark is used ...

- after a word, phrase, or sentence that expresses strong feeling
- inside quotation marks when the quotation is an exclamation

Quotation marks are used ...

- to set off a direct quotation—a person's exact words (single quotation marks are used for quotes within quotes.)
- to enclose titles of articles, short stories, poems, songs and other parts of books and periodicals

Underlining (italics) is used ...

- for titles of books, plays, magazines, newspapers, films, ships, radio and TV programs, music albums, works of art
- to emphasize words, letters, and figures referred to as such and for foreign words

QUICK REFERENCE CHART

Fraction-Stick Chart

Use this Fraction-Stick Chart to find equivalent fractions, determine which of two fractions is larger, and compare fractions. You may want to make a copy of this fraction stick chart and cut the fraction bars apart to use them with your work.

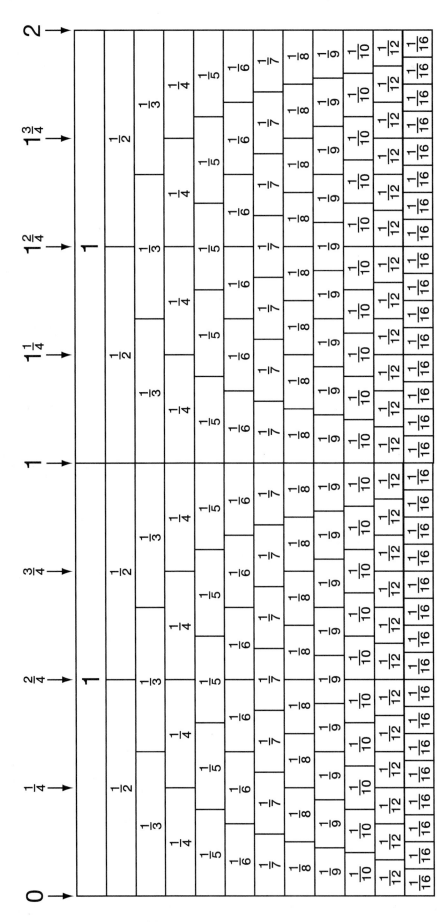

QUICK REFERENCE CHART

NORTH AMERICA

Country	Capital
Antigua & Barbuda	St. John's
Aruba	Oranjestad
Bahamas	Nassau
Barbados	Bridgetown
Bermuda	Hamilton
British Virgin Islands	Road Town
Canada	Ottawa
Cayman Islands	George Town
Cuba	Havana
Dominica	Roseau
Dominican Republic	Santo Domingo
Greenland	Godthåb (Nuuk)
Grenada	St. George's
Guadeloupe	Basse-Terre
Haiti	Port-au-Prince
Jamaica	Kingston
Martinique	Fort-de-France
Montserrat	Plymouth
Netherlands Antilles	Willemstad
Puerto Rico	San Juan
Saint Kitts & Nevis	Basseterre
Saint Lucia	Castries
St. Pierre & Miquelon	St. Pierre
St. Vincent & Grenadines	Kingstown
Trinidad & Tobago	Port-of-Spain
Turks & Caicos Islands	Grand Turk
United States	Washington, D.C.
Virgin Islands of U.S.	Charlotte Amalie

CANADA 🍁

Province	Capital
Alberta	Edmonton
British Columbia	Victoria
Manitoba	Winnipeg
New Brunswick	Fredericton
Newfoundland and Labrador	St. John's
Nova Scotia	Halifax
Ontario	Toronto
Prince Edward Island	Charlottetown
Quebec	Quebec
Saskatchewan	Regina

Territory	Capital
Northwest Territories	Yellowknife
Yukon Territories	Whitehorse

CENTRAL AMERICA

Country	Capital
Belize	Belmopan
Costa Rica	San Jose
El Salvador	San Salvador
Guatemala	Guatemala City
Honduras	Tegucigalpa
Mexico	Mexico City
Nicaragua	Managua
Panama	Panama City

SOUTH AMERICA

Country	Capital
Argentina	Buenos Aires
Bolivia	La Paz/Sucre
Brazil	Brasilia
Chile	Santiago
Colombia	Bogota
Ecuador	Quito
Falkland Island	Stanley
French Guiana	Cayenne
Guyana	Georgetown
Paraguay	Asuncion
Peru	Lima
Suriname	Paramaribo
Uruguay	Montevideo
Venezuela	Caracas

QUICK REFERENCE CHART

EUROPE

Country	Capital
Albania	Tirane
Andorra	Andorra la Vella
Armenia	Yerevan
Austria	Vienna
Azerbaijan	Baku
Belarus	Minsk
Belgium	Brussels
Bosnia-Herzegovina	Sarajevo
Bulgaria	Sofia
Croatia	Zagreb
Czech Republic	Prague
Denmark	Copenhagen
Estonia	Tallinn
Finland	Helsinki
France	Paris
Georgia	Tbilisi
Germany	Berlin
Gibraltar	Gibraltar
Greece	Athens
Hungary	Budapest
Iceland	Reykjavik
Ireland	Dublin
Italy	Rome
Latvia	Riga
Liechtenstein	Vaduz
Lithuania	Vilnius
Luxembourg	Luxembourg
Macedonia	Skopje
Malta	Valletta
Moldova	Kishinev
Monaco	Monaco
Netherlands, The	Amsterdam
Norway	Oslo
Poland	Warsaw
Portugal	Lisbon
Romania	Bucharest
Russia	Moscow
San Marino	San Marino
Slovakia	Bratislava
Slovenia	Ljubljana
Spain	Madrid
Sweden	Stockholm
Switzerland	Bern
Ukraine	Kiev
United Kingdom	London
Vatican City	Vatican City
Yugoslavia	Belgrade

UNITED STATES

State	Capital
Alabama	Montgomery
Alaska	Juneau
Arizona	Phoenix
Arkansas	Little Rock
California	Sacramento
Colorado	Denver
Connecticut	Hartford
Delaware	Dover
Florida	Tallahassee
Georgia	Atlanta
Hawaii	Honolulu
Idaho	Boise
Illinois	Springfield
Indiana	Indianapolis
Iowa	Des Moines
Kansas	Topeka
Kentucky	Frankfort
Louisiana	Baton Rouge
Maine	Augusta
Maryland	Annapolis
Massachusetts	Boston
Michigan	Lansing
Minnesota	St. Paul
Mississippi	Jackson
Missouri	Jefferson City
Montana	Helena
Nebraska	Lincoln
Nevada	Carson City
New Hampshire	Concord
New Jersey	Trenton
New Mexico	Santa Fe
New York	Albany
North Carolina	Raleigh
North Dakota	Bismarck
Ohio	Columbus
Oklahoma	Oklahoma City
Oregon	Salem
Pennsylvania	Harrisburg
Rhode Island	Providence
South Carolina	Columbia
South Dakota	Pierre
Tennessee	Nashville
Texas	Austin
Utah	Salt Lake City
Vermont	Montpelier
Virginia	Richmond
Washington	Olympia
West Virginia	Charleston
Wisconsin	Madison
Wyoming	Cheyenne

Notes

_____
_____
_____
_____
_____
_____
_____
_____
_____
_____
_____
_____
_____
_____
_____
_____
_____
_____
_____
_____

5 Five things I'm thankful for:

1._____
2._____
3._____
4._____
5._____

Notes

_____
_____
_____
_____
_____
_____
_____
_____
_____
_____
_____
_____
_____
_____
_____
_____
_____
_____

5 Five things I'm thankful for:

1._____
2._____
3._____
4._____
5._____

Notes

_____
_____
_____
_____
_____
_____
_____
_____
_____
_____
_____
_____
_____
_____
_____
_____
_____
_____
_____
_____

5 Five things I'm thankful for:

1._____
2._____
3._____
4._____
5._____

Notes

_____
_____
_____
_____
_____
_____
_____
_____
_____
_____
_____
_____
_____
_____
_____
_____
_____

5 Five things I'm thankful for:

1._____
2._____
3._____
4._____
5._____

Notes

_____
_____
_____
_____
_____
_____
_____
_____
_____
_____
_____
_____
_____
_____
_____
_____
_____
_____
_____
_____

5 Five things I'm thankful for:

1._____
2._____
3._____
4._____
5._____

Notes

_____
_____
_____
_____
_____
_____
_____
_____
_____
_____
_____
_____
_____
_____
_____
_____
_____
_____

5 Five things I'm thankful for:

1. _____
2. _____
3. _____
4. _____
5. _____

Better Bodies   Better Behavior

Up until now, **Summer Bridge Activities**™ has been all about your mind...

But the other parts of you—who you are, how you act, and how you feel—are important too. These pages are all about helping build a better you this summer.

Keeping your body strong and healthy helps you live better, learn better, and feel better. To keep your body healthy, you need to do things like eat right, get enough sleep, and exercise. The Physical Fitness pages of Building Better Bodies will teach you about good eating habits and the importance of proper exercise. You can even train for a Presidential Fitness Award over the summer.

The Character pages are all about building a better you on the inside. They've got fun activities for you and your family to do together. The activities will help you develop important values and habits you'll need as you grow up.

After a summer of Building Better Bodies and Behavior and **Summer Bridge Activities**™, there may be a whole new you ready for school in the fall!

• •

For Parents: Introduction to Character Education

Character education is simply giving your child clear messages about the values you and your family consider important. Many studies have shown that a basic core of values is universal. You will find certain values reflected in the laws of every country and incorporated in the teachings of religious, ethical, and other belief systems throughout the world.

The character activities included here are designed to span the entire summer. Each week your child will be introduced to a new value, with a quote and two activities that illustrate it. Research has shown that character education is most effective when parents reinforce the values in their child's daily routine; therefore, we encourage parents to be involved as their child completes the lessons.

Here are some suggestions on how to maximize these lessons.
• Read through the lesson yourself. Then set aside a block of time for you and your child to discuss the value.
• Plan a block of time to work on the suggested activities.
• Discuss the meaning of the quote with your child. Ask, "What do you think the quote means?" Have your child ask other members of the family the same question. If possible, include grandparents, aunts, uncles, and cousins.
• Use the quote as often as you can during the week. You'll be pleasantly surprised to learn that both you and your child will have it memorized by the end of the week.
• For extra motivation, you can set a reward for completing each week's activities.
• Point out to your child other people who are actively displaying a value. Example: "See how John is helping Mrs. Olsen by raking her leaves."
• Be sure to praise your child each time he or she practices a value: "Mary, it was very courteous of you to wait until I finished speaking."
• Find time in your day to talk about values. Turn off the radio in the car and chat with your children; take a walk in the evening as a family; read a story about the weekly value at bedtime; or give a back rub while you talk about what makes your child happy or sad.
• Finally, model the values you want your child to acquire. Remember, children will do as you do, not as you say.

Name _____   Date _____

How I Measure Up!

You will be filling in this page twice—once now and once at the end of the summer to see how you have grown. Have an adult help you measure yourself to fill in the blanks below.

around the neck ____/____

smile ____/____

neck to belly button ____/____

around the wrist ____/____

shoulder to elbow ____/____

elbow to wrist ____/____

around the waist ____/____

length of longest finger ____/____

waist to ankle ____/____

around the knee ____/____

foot length ____/____

around the ankle ____/____

around the neck ____/____

smile ____/____

neck to belly button ____/____

around the wrist ____/____

shoulder to elbow ____/____

elbow to wrist ____/____

around the waist ____/____

length of longest finger ____/____

waist to ankle ____/____

around the knee ____/____

foot length ____/____

around the ankle ____/____

Building Better Bodies and Behavior

128

© **Summer Bridge Activities**™

Nutrition

The food you eat helps your body grow. It gives you energy to work and play. Some foods give you protein or fats. Other foods provide vitamins, minerals, or carbohydrates. These are all things your body needs. Eating a variety of good foods each day will help you stay healthy. How much and what foods you need depends on many things, including whether you're a girl or boy, how active you are, and how old you are. To figure out the right amount of food for you, go to http://www.mypyramid.gov/mypyramid/index.aspx and use the Pyramid Plan Calculator. In the meantime, here are some general guidelines.

Your body needs nutrients from each food group every day.

Grains	Vegetables	Fruits	Oils	Milk	Meat & Beans
4 to 5 ounce equivalents each day (an ounce might be a slice of bread, a packet of oatmeal, or a bowl of cereal)	1 1/2 cups each day	1 to 1 1/2 cups each day		1 to 2 cups of milk (or other calcium-rich food) each day	3 to 5 ounce equivalents each day

What foods did you eat today?

Which food group did you eat the most foods from today?

From which food group did you eat the least?

Which meal included the most food groups?

Meal Planning

Plan out three balanced meals for one day. Arrange your meals so that by the end of the day, you will have had all the recommended amounts of food from each food group listed on the food pyramid.

Breakfast

_____

_____

_____

_____

Lunch

_____

_____

_____

_____

Dinner

_____

_____

_____

_____

Meal Tracker

Use these charts to record the amount of food you eat from each food group for one or two weeks. Have another family member keep track, too, and compare.

	Grains	Milk	Meat & Beans	Fruits	Vegetables	Oils/ Sweets
Monday						
Tuesday						
Wednesday						
Thursday						
Friday						
Saturday						
Sunday						

	Grains	Milk	Meat & Beans	Fruits	Vegetables	Oils/ Sweets
Monday						
Tuesday						
Wednesday						
Thursday						
Friday						
Saturday						
Sunday						

	Grains	Milk	Meat & Beans	Fruits	Vegetables	Oils/ Sweets
Monday						
Tuesday						
Wednesday						
Thursday						
Friday						
Saturday						
Sunday						

	Grains	Milk	Meat & Beans	Fruits	Vegetables	Oils/ Sweets
Monday						
Tuesday						
Wednesday						
Thursday						
Friday						
Saturday						
Sunday						

Get Moving!

Did you know that getting no exercise can be almost as bad for you as smoking? So get moving this summer!

Summer is the perfect time to get out and get in shape. Your fitness program should include three parts:

- Get 30 minutes of aerobic exercise per day, three to five days a week.

- Exercise your muscles to improve strength and flexibility.

- Make it FUN! Do things that you like to do. Include your friends and family.

Couch Potato Quiz

1. Name three things you do each day that get you moving.

2. Name three things you do a few times a week that are good exercise.

3. How many hours do you spend each week playing outside or exercising?

4. How much TV do you watch each day?

5. How much time do you spend playing computer or video games?

If the time you spend on activities 4 and 5 adds up to more than you spend on 1–3, you could be headed for a spud's life!

You can find information on fitness at
www.fitness.gov or www.kidshealth.org

Activity Pyramid

The Activity Pyramid works like the Food Pyramid. You can use the Activity Pyramid to help plan your summer exercise program. Fill in the blanks below.

List 1 thing that isn't good exercise that you could do less of this summer.

1. _____

List 3 fun activities you enjoy that get you moving and are good exercise.

1. gymnastics
2. Volleyball
3. Swimming

List 3 exercises you could do to build strength and flexibility this summer.

1. swim
2. runing
3. sports

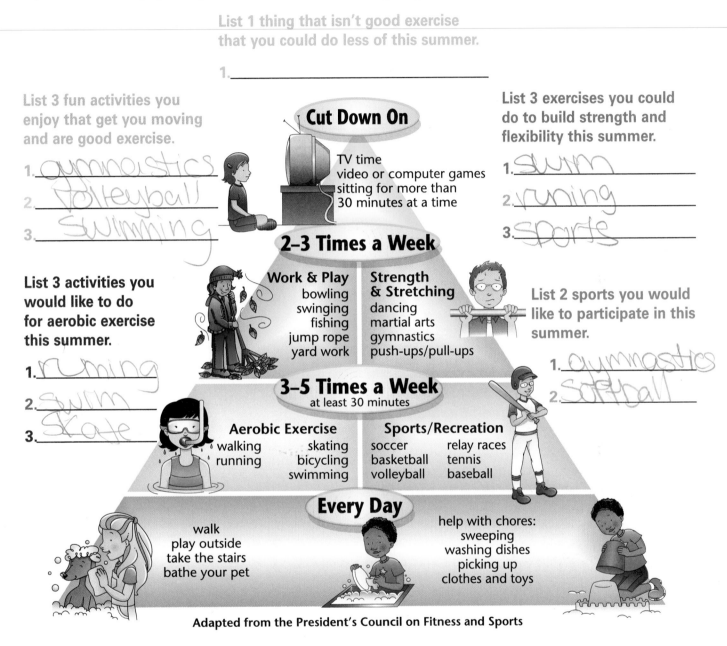

Cut Down On

TV time
video or computer games
sitting for more than
30 minutes at a time

2–3 Times a Week

Work & Play
bowling
swinging
fishing
jump rope
yard work

Strength & Stretching
dancing
martial arts
gymnastics
push-ups/pull-ups

List 3 activities you would like to do for aerobic exercise this summer.

1. runing
2. swim
3. skate

List 2 sports you would like to participate in this summer.

1. gymnastics
2. softball

3–5 Times a Week
at least 30 minutes

Aerobic Exercise
walking   skating
running   bicycling
             swimming

Sports/Recreation
soccer   relay races
basketball   tennis
volleyball   baseball

Every Day

walk
play outside
take the stairs
bathe your pet

help with chores:
sweeping
washing dishes
picking up
clothes and toys

Adapted from the President's Council on Fitness and Sports

List 5 everyday things you can do to get moving more often.

1. stairs
2. work out
3. healthy food
4. 30 mm off t.v.
5. 9 hrs of sleep

Fitness Fundamentals

Basic physical fitness includes several things:

Cardiovascular Endurance. Your cardiovascular system includes your heart and blood vessels. You need a strong heart to pump your blood which delivers oxygen and nutrients to your body.

Muscular Strength. This is how strong your muscles are.

Muscular Endurance. Endurance has to do with how long you can use your muscles before they get tired.

Flexibility. This is your ability to move your joints and to use your muscles through their full range of motion.

Body Composition. Your body is made up of lean mass and fat mass.

Lean mass includes the water, muscles, tissues, and organs in your body.

Fat mass includes the fat your body stores for energy. Exercise helps you burn body fat and maintain good body composition.

The goal of a summer fitness program is to improve in all the areas of physical fitness.

You build cardiovascular endurance through **aerobic** exercise. For **aerobic** exercise, you need to work large muscle groups at a steady pace. This increases your heart rate and breathing. You can jog, walk, hike, swim, dance, do aerobics, ride a bike, go rowing, climb stairs, rollerblade, play golf, backpack…

You should get at least 30 minutes of aerobic exercise per day, three to five days a week.

You build muscular strength and endurance with exercises that work your muscles, like sit-ups, push-ups, pull-ups, and weight lifting.

You can increase flexibility through stretching exercises. These are good for warm-ups, too.

Find these fitness words.

Word Bank

aerobic	exercise	fat
muscular	flexible	blood
endurance	strength	oxygen
heart rate	joint	hiking

```
u a e y i d t y a g d x p o b
o l s h s t r e n g t h l r c
e w l o o o z v s d m i h d t
g t z w s j o i n t m n k a o
s q a c h i p s a d e t f f m
k c q r x i q f l e x i b l e
e e j o t v k w t e u r g e g
i e s e d r v i n t n f k x o
k e l i d c a d n n e g e j w
u z e d c y u e i g g x i c i
j c i b o r e a h h y w v s i
a m r a a c e m x x x y d i g
f p v n p n d x u s o x e f k
p o c b l o o d e g z a x m c
l e m u s c u l a r m k g i s
```

134

Your Summer Fitness Program

Start your summer fitness program by choosing at least one aerobic activity from your Activity Pyramid. You can choose more than one for variety.

_____ _____ _____

Do this activity three to five times each week. Keep it up for at least 30 minutes each time.
(Exercise hard enough to increase your heart rate and your breathing. Don't exercise so hard that you get dizzy or can't catch your breath.)

Use this chart to plan when you will exercise, or use it as a record when you exercise.

DATE	ACTIVITY	TIME
6/8	Kickball	60min

DATE	ACTIVITY	TIME

Plan a reward for meeting your exercise goals for two weeks.
(You can make copies of this chart to track your fitness all summer long.)

Start Slow!

Remember to start out slow. Exercise is about getting stronger. It's not about being superman—or superwoman—right off the bat.

   Building Better Bodies and Behavior

Are You Up to the Challenge?

The Presidential Physical Fitness Award Program was designed to help kids get into shape and have fun. To earn the award, you take five fitness tests. These are usually given by teachers at school, but you can train for them this summer. Make a chart to track your progress. Keep working all summer to see if you can improve your score.

Remember: Start Slow!

1. Curl-ups. Lie on the floor with your knees bent and your feet about 12 inches from your buttocks. Cross your arms over your chest. Raise your trunk up and touch your elbows to your thighs. Do as many as you can in one minute.

2. Shuttle Run. Draw a starting line. Put two blocks 30 feet away. Run the 30 feet, pick up a block, and bring it back to the starting line. Then run and bring back the second block. Record your fastest time.

3. V-sit Reach. Sit on the floor with your legs straight and your feet 8 to 12 inches apart. Put a ruler between your feet, pointing past your toes. Have a partner hold your legs straight, and keep your toes pointed up. Link your thumbs together and reach forward, palms down, as far as you can along the ruler.

4. One-Mile Walk/Run. On a track or some safe area, run one mile. You can walk as often as you need to. Finish as fast as possible. (Ages six to seven may want to run a quarter mile; ages eight to nine, half a mile.)

5. Pull-ups. Grip a bar with an overhand grip (the backs of your hands toward your face). Have someone lift you up if you need help. Hang with your arms and legs straight. Pull your body up until your chin is over the bar; then let yourself back down. Do as many as you can.

Respect

Respect is showing good manners toward all people, not just those you know or who are like you. Respect is treating everyone, no matter what religion, race, or culture, male or female, rich or poor, in a way that you would want to be treated. The easiest way to do this is to decide to **never** take part in activities and to **never** use words that make fun of people because they are different from you or your friends.

It's not necessary for eagles to be crows.
What I am, I am.
~ Sitting Bull

Word Search

Find these words that also mean *respect*.

Word Bank

honor
idolize
admire
worship
recognize
appreciate
venerate
prize

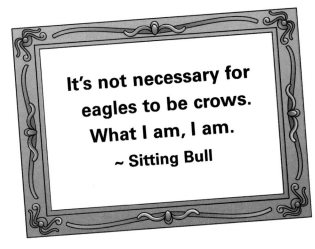

```
m c e t a r e n e v
w j t a h p s e p t
e c a d n n t z i w
z v i m w u k i h r
i e c i h b h n s o
l z e r v b j g r n
o i r e k a u o o o
d r p g m e e c w h
i p p b g c h e r j
q f a b f g u r r z
```

Activity

This week go to the library and check out *The Well: David's Story* by Mildred Taylor (1995). The story is set in Mississippi in the early 1900s and tells about David's family, who shares their well with both black and white neighbors. Be sure to read this book with your parents.

Gratitude

Gratitude is when you thank people for the good things they have given you or done for you. Thinking about people and events in your life that make you feel grateful (thankful) will help you become a happier person.

There are over 465 different ways of saying thank you. Here are a few:

Danke   Toda   Merci   Gracias   **Nandri**

Spasibo   Arigato   **Gadda ge**   Paldies   Hvala

Make a list of ten things you are grateful for.

1. _____
2. _____
3. _____
4. _____
5. _____

6. _____
7. _____
8. _____
9. _____
10. _____

A Recipe for Saying Thanks

1. Make a colorful card.
2. On the inside, write a thank-you note to someone who has done something nice for you.
3. Address an envelope to that person.
4. Pick out a cool stamp.
5. Drop your note in the nearest mailbox.

Saying thank you creates love.

~ Daphne Rose Kingma

Manners

If you were the only person in the world, you wouldn't have to have **good manners** or be **courteous**. However, there are over six billion people on our planet, and good manners help us all get along with each other.

Children with good manners are usually well liked by other children and are certainly liked by adults. Here are some simple rules for good manners:
- When you ask for something, say, "Please."
- When someone gives you something, say, "Thank you."
- When someone says, "Thank you," say, "You're welcome."
- If you walk in front of someone or bump into a person, say, "Excuse me."
- When someone else is talking, wait before speaking.
- Share and take turns.

No kindness, no matter how small, is ever wasted. ~ Aesop's Fables

Find these words or phrases that deal with _courtesy_.

Word Bank

etiquette
thank you
welcome
excuse me
please
share
turns
patience
polite
manners

m	u	o	y	k	n	a	h	t
e	m	o	c	l	e	w	e	e
e	s	a	e	l	p	x	f	c
a	m	q	u	f	c	x	r	n
e	t	t	e	u	q	i	t	e
s	r	g	s	n	r	u	t	i
s	r	e	n	n	a	m	g	t
v	m	p	o	l	i	t	e	a
e	i	e	r	a	h	s	h	p

I've Got Manners

Make a colorful poster to display on your bedroom door or on the refrigerator. List five ways you are going to practice your manners. Be creative and decorate with watercolors, poster paints, pictures cut from magazines, clip art, or geometric shapes.

Instead of making a poster, you could make a mobile to hang from your ceiling that shows five different manners to practice.

Consequences

A **consequence** is what happens after you choose to do something. Some choices lead to good consequences. Other choices lead to bad consequences. An example of this would be choosing whether to eat an apple or a bag of potato chips. The potato chips might seem like a more tasty snack, but eating an apple is better for your body. Or, you may not like to do your homework, but if you choose not to, you won't do well in school, and you may not be able to go out with your friends.

It's hard to look into the future and see how a choice will influence what happens today, tomorrow, or years from now. But whenever we choose to do something, there are consequences that go with our choice. That's why it is important to *think before you choose.*

Remember: The easiest choice does not always lead to the best consequence.

We choose to go to the moon not because it's easy, but because it's hard.
~ John F. Kennedy

Activity

Get a copy of *The Tale of Peter Rabbit* by Beatrix Potter. This simple story is full of choices that lead to bad consequences. Write down three choices Peter made and the consequences that occurred. Who made a good choice, and what was the consequence?

Find these words that also mean *consequence.*

Word Bank		
result	outcome	fallout
payoff	effect	reaction
product	aftermath	upshot

```
b e h p j c p o j q
i t h a e l r w r v
z u t y f r o s t v
g o a o f e d t o m
r l m f e a u r h j
e l r f c c c e s e
s a e b t t t m p g
u f t s e i j t u i
l e f e m o c t u o
t c a i m n o h f d
```

Friendship

Friends come in all sizes, shapes, and ages: brothers, sisters, parents, neighbors, good teachers, and school and sports friends.

There is a saying, "To have a friend you need to be a friend." Can you think of a day when someone might have tried to get you to say or do unkind things to someone else? Sometimes it takes courage to be a real friend. Did you have the courage to say no?

A Recipe for Friendship

1 cup of always listening to ideas and stories
2 pounds of never talking behind a friend's back
1 pound of no mean teasing
2 cups of always helping a friend who needs help

Take these ingredients and mix completely together. Add laughter, kindness, hugs, and even tears. Bake for as long as it takes to make your friendship good and strong.

I get by with a little
help from my friends.
~ John Lennon

Family Night at the Movies

Rent *Toy Story* or *Toy Story II*. Each movie is a simple, yet powerful, tale about true friendship. Fix a big bowl of popcorn to share with your family during the show.

International Friendship Day

The first Sunday in August is International Friendship Day. This is a perfect day to remember all your friends and how they have helped you during your friendship. Give your friends a call or send them an email or snail-mail card.

Confidence

People are **confident** or have **confidence** when they feel like they can succeed at a certain task. To feel confident about doing something, most people need to practice a task over and over.

Reading, pitching a baseball, writing in cursive, playing the flute, even mopping a floor are all examples of tasks that need to be practiced before people feel confident they can succeed.

What are five things you feel confident doing?

What is one thing you want to feel more confident doing?

Make a plan for how and when you will practice until you feel confident.

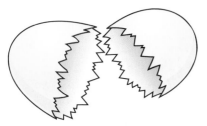

You Crack Me Up!

Materials needed:
1 dozen eggs
a mixing bowl

Cracking eggs without breaking the yolk or getting egg whites all over your hands takes practice.

1. Watch an adult break an egg into the bowl. How did they hold their hands? How did they pull the egg apart?

2. Now you try. Did you do a perfect job the first time? Keep trying until you begin to feel confident about cracking eggs.

3. Use the eggs immediately to make a cheese omelet or custard pie. Refrigerate any unused eggs for up to three days.

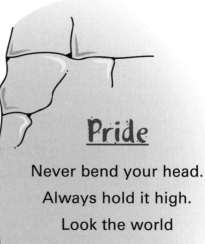

Pride

Never bend your head.

Always hold it high.

Look the world

Right in the eye.

~ Helen Keller

Responsibility

You show **responsibility** by doing what you agree or promise to do. It might be a task, such as a homework assignment, or a chore, such as feeding your fish.

When you are young, your parents and teachers will give you simple tasks like putting away toys or brushing your teeth without being asked. As you get older, you will be given more responsibility. You might be trusted to come home from a friend's house at a certain time or drive to the store for groceries.

It takes a lot of practice to grow up to be a responsible person. The easiest way to practice is by keeping your promises and doing what you know is right.

A parent is responsible for different things than a child or a teenager. Write three activities you are responsible for every day. Then write three things a parent is responsible for every day.

If you want your eggs hatched, sit on them yourself. ~ Haitian Proverb

Activity

Materials needed:
21 pennies or counters such as beans, rocks, or marbles
2 small containers labeled #1 and #2

Decide on a reward for successfully completing this activity.
Put all the counters in container #1.
Review the three activities you are responsible for every day.
Each night before you go to bed, put one counter for each completed activity into container #2. At the end of seven days count all the counters in container #2.
If you have 16 or more counters in container #2, you are on your way to becoming very responsible. Collect your reward.

My reward is_____.

Service/Helping

Service is **helping** another person or group of people without asking for any kind of reward or payment. These are some good things that happen when you do service:

1. You feel closer to the people in your community (neighborhood).
2. You feel pride in yourself when you see that you can help other people in need.
3. Your family feels proud of you.
4. You will make new friends as you help others.

An old saying goes, "Charity begins at home." This means that you don't have to do big, important-sounding things to help people. You can start in your own home and neighborhood.

Activity

Each day this week, do one act of service around your house. Don't ask for or take any kind of payment or reward. Be creative! Possible acts of service are

1. Carry in the groceries, do the dishes, or fold the laundry.
2. Read aloud to a younger brother or sister.
3. Make breakfast or pack lunches.
4. Recycle newspapers and cans.
5. Clean the refrigerator or your room.

At the end of the week, think of a project to do with your family that will help your community. You could play musical instruments or sing at a nursing home, set up a lemonade stand and give the money you make to the Special Olympics, offer to play board games with children in the hospital, or pick some flowers and take them to a neighbor. The list goes on and on.

> **All the flowers of tomorrow are in the seeds of today.**
> ~ Indian Proverb

Word Search

Find these words that also mean *service*.

Word Bank		
help	assist	aid
charity	support	boost
benefit	contribute	guide

m	v	l	a	o	d	w	f	d	r
c	o	n	t	r	i	b	u	t	e
t	b	s	x	c	a	z	v	x	q
s	g	p	q	g	w	b	n	y	t
i	v	l	y	g	u	v	x	z	i
s	n	e	t	e	x	m	n	m	f
s	f	h	d	u	d	g	t	e	e
a	u	c	h	a	r	i	t	y	n
s	u	p	p	o	r	t	u	x	e
b	o	o	s	t	g	f	j	g	b

Honesty and Trust

Being an **honest** person means you don't steal, cheat, or tell lies. **Trust** is when you believe someone will be honest. If you are dishonest, or not truthful, people will not trust you.

You want to tell the truth because it is important to have your family and friends trust you. However, it takes courage to tell the truth, especially if you don't want people to get mad at you or be disappointed in the way you behaved.

How would your parents feel if you lied to them? People almost always find out about lies, and most parents will be more angry about a lie than if you had told them the truth in the first place.

When family or friends ask about something, remember that honesty is telling the truth. Honesty is telling what really happened. Honesty is keeping your promises. *Be proud of being an honest person.*

Write down five feeling words about how you felt when you *weren't* honest or trusted.

1
2
3
4
5

Write down five feeling words about how you felt when you *were* honest or trusted.

1
2
3
4
5

Parent note: Help your child by pointing out times he or she acted honestly.

Count to Ten

Tape ten pieces of colored paper to your refrigerator. For one week, each time you tell the truth or keep a promise, take one piece of paper down and put it in the recycling bin. If all ten pieces of paper are gone by the end of the week, collect your reward.

Most Improved

Honesty is the first chapter in the book of wisdom.
~Thomas Jefferson

My reward is _____.

Happiness

Happiness is a feeling that comes when you enjoy your life. Different things make different people happy. Some people feel happy when they are playing soccer. Other people feel happy when they are playing the cello. It is important to understand what makes you happy so you can include some of these things in your daily plan.

These are some actions that show you are happy: laughing, giggling, skipping, smiling, and hugging.

Make a list of five activities that make you feel happy.

1
2
3
4
5

Bonus!

List two things you could do to make someone else happy.

1._____

2._____

Activity

Write down a plan to do one activity each day this week that makes you happy.

Try simple things—listen to your favorite song, play with a friend, bake muffins, shoot hoops, etc.

Be sure to thank everyone who helps you, and don't forget to laugh!

Happy Thought

The world is so full

of a number of things,

I'm sure we should

all be happy as kings.

~Robert Louis Stevenson

Notes

_____
_____
_____
_____
_____
_____
_____
_____
_____
_____
_____
_____
_____
_____
_____
_____
_____

5 Five things I'm thankful for:

1._____
2._____
3._____
4._____
5._____

Notes

_____
_____
_____
_____
_____
_____
_____
_____
_____
_____
_____
_____
_____
_____

5 Five things I'm thankful for:

1._____
2._____
3._____
4._____
5._____

Notes

_____
_____
_____
_____
_____
_____
_____
_____
_____
_____
_____
_____
_____
_____
_____
_____
_____

5 Five things I'm thankful for:

1. _____
2. _____
3. _____
4. _____
5. _____

Notes

_____
_____
_____
_____
_____
_____
_____
_____
_____
_____
_____
_____
_____
_____
_____
_____
_____
_____

5 Five things I'm thankful for:

1. _____
2. _____
3. _____
4. _____
5. _____

Certificate of Completion

your name

HAS COMPLETED

Summer Bridge Activities™

AND IS READY FOR THE 7TH GRADE!

Ms. Hansen

Ms. Hansen

Mr. Fredrickson

Mr. Fredrickson

Parent's Signature

www.SUMMER BRIDGE ACTIVITIES.com